Perspectives on Nepal

Perspectives on Nepal

Recent History and Indo-Nepal Relations

Deb Mukharji

SHIPRA

INDIAN COUNCIL OF WORLD AFFAIRS

ISBN: 978-81-7541-866-0

First Published in India in 2016

Perspectives on Nepal: Recent History and Indo-Nepal Relations

Published by:
SHIPRA PUBLICATIONS
LG 18-19, Pankaj Central Market
I.P. Ext., Patparganj, Delhi 110092, India
Tel.: +91 11 2223 5152/6152
E-mail: info@shiprapublication.com
www.shiprapublication.com

Acknowledgements

I would like to express my most sincere gratitude to all those in Nepal, from politics, academia, journalism and in private life who have greatly enriched my understanding of the evolving politics of Nepal, as also Indo-Nepal relations. My conclusions may, at times, be different from theirs, but for that I remain solely responsible. I remain grateful to friends in India who have gone through the manuscript and made most valuable suggestions.

I am deeply thankful to Uddhab Pyakurel and Abhijit Dihidar, research scholars at Jawaharlal Nehru University from Nepal and India, who delved untiringly into books and documents to provide me much more than background information.

Lastly, I am grateful to the Indian Council of World Affairs for its support and assistance in completing the monograph. Without the encouragement of the then Director General, the project may never have been undertaken.

Contents

Introduction

For the past several years, since the *janā andolan* of 2006, it has been a common refrain to claim that Nepal is in a state of flux, or that a 'new' Nepal is about to emerge. Depending on one's level of optimism, one could foresee some levelling of the apparent deep divides between political parties or, conversely, an unending saga of moves and counter moves while governance flagged and the economy staggered. Earlier, from around 2001, when politics was subject to the whims of the palace and large numbers died in the countryside during the Maoist insurgency, there had been years of dark despair when no glimmer of light could be seen at the end of the blood-soaked tunnel. Hence, there was optimism when insurgents agreed with the mainstream political parties to be part of a democratic framework, the palace retreated, and people's power seemed to have triumphed. As the years passed, however, political calculations gradually overtook political vision and today, in the middle of 2013, Nepal continues to seek a road map for the future. The excitement and the anticipation of the period following the end of the armed conflict in Nepal has given way to a sense of ennui and déjà vu as Nepal's political classes continue to engage in inter and intra party manipulations for power.

It is not only foreign observers who may lose their way in the maze of Nepal's politics and society. An eminent Nepali academic and analyst wrote recently, "Theorising Nepali politics is a daunting task. Politics ordained by constraints of tradition and history, political culture embedded in past traditions, societal construct, and primordial loyalties with a modern mix have made it imponderable. So it is full of enigmas and paradoxes that provide us with deceptive political scenarios" *(Lok Raj Baral, Nepal — Nation State in the Wilderness, Sage 2012).*

Besides, Nepal has been undergoing multiple revolutions simultaneously. There has been the end of a monarchy which, besides the divinity attributed to it, the people had been taught to consider as not only representing, but subsuming the state. A nation identified with the person of the monarch has to find a new basis for nationhood. A feudal order that flowed from the palace and inculcated attitudes of subservience, which lasted for over two centuries, has given way to an explosion of long-suppressed aspirations. The attenuated democracy achieved in 1990 is being sought to be converted into a system that may truly reflect the wishes of the people.

If there is dismay in Nepal, and among well wishers of the Nepali people, that a promised or expected transition to a 'new' Nepal remains mired in a state of political uncertainty, it must be tempered by the recognition that over the past couple of decades, Nepal has witnessed unparalleled extremes of violence and is attempting a transition to democracy that comes, perhaps, only once in the life of a nation. And despite the challenges, the basic infrastructure of the establishment, including the judiciary and the armed forces, have maintained their integrity.

The evolution of Nepal from a feudal polity into modern society was possible even five decades ago if the first experiment with democracy had not been suppressed by royal decree in 1960 when the first elected parliament was dismissed, followed by three decades of '*panchayati raj*', which was, effectively, rule by the palace, its courtiers and favourites. It was paternalistic with a strong tinge of preserving the *status quo.* The people's uprising of 1990 and the constitution that followed resulted in elected governments in a multi-party democracy. But even as the elected governments over the next decade attempted to bring about some changes in the nature of governance, they had to face the twin challenges of the Maoist insurgency and a palace unreconciled to rule by the representatives of the people. There was, apparently, a mutually shared desire between the extreme right and the extreme left, the palace and the Maoists to discredit the political parties representing the centre. The intra and inter party differences and manipulations led to successive changes of government, with focus straying from national issues. There was little effort to address the aspirations and concerns of marginalized groups with either understanding or commitment. Thus, while mainstream political parties may be legitimately charged with not addressing the long-standing core concerns of the people, the fact also remains that the "people's war" was started before they had an adequate period for delivery and that the palace was deep into discrediting them. Also, the Maoists had decided long ago, after the first *jana andolan* had ended, that they would pursue, if necessary, a path of violence for attaining their objectives. The recent breakaway Maoist party of Mohan Vaidya and others seeks a committed continuation of that policy.

Starting in 1996, the Maoist insurgency took a heavy toll in lives and ravaged the lives of uncounted numbers in the countryside. The number of 17,000 killed in ten years in a population of twenty five million is staggering enough, but beyond this statistic also lies the widespread disruption of the lives of citizens. The insurgents and the army were both guilty of targeting common citizens, and not merely their adversaries, in an effort to prevail by terror. As civil society activists do not fail to point out, neither of the parties involved are anxious to render an accounting of those years.

The massacre at Narayanhiti palace by a demented prince was a crucial turning point in the history of Nepal. The horror of the event besides, it brought to the throne Gyanendra Shah, brother of the late king, who failed entirely in providing sober counsel and guidance to a nation in emotional turmoil and distress. His inherent contempt for the political classes, and misplaced confidence in his own powers of manipulation, led inexorably to his palace coup of February, 2005, through which he converted his own position as the CEO of Nepal. The rest is history, and history shall judge that the end of the monarchy established by Prithvi Narayan Shah was due to not primarily the Maoists or the parliament, but the misguided actions of the last royal occupant of Narayanhiti.

It used to be said in the late 90s that there were three major forces in Nepali politics: the mainstream political parties, the palace, and the Maoists. A triangular conflict of interests, as was in evidence during 1996-2005, could indefinitely postpone a return to stability. But a joining of forces between any two would marginalize the third. The palace had been in intermittent touch with the Maoists through the 90s during King Birendra's time with a view to neutralize the mainstream democratic parties and unwilling to choose a military solution to the insurgency. Under King Gyanendra, parliament became a casualty with his proclamation of October 4, 2002, by which the prime minister was dismissed for incompetence, parliamentary elections postponed indefinitely, and the king assumed executive powers. There followed a period of musical chairs in the post of appointed prime ministers until February 1, 2005, when pretensions were cast aside and the king assumed full control of the government. This measure faced the democratic centre as well as the Maoists with the prospect of a return to the twilight years initiated by King Mahendra in 1960. Two of the three contending parties in the polity of Nepal came together to forge a common understanding under the 12 Point Agreement of November, 2005. Neither threats nor promises from the palace bore fruit and the denouement came with *jana andolan II* of April, 2006.

The elections of 2008 followed a series of understandings between the mainstream political parties and the Maoists. The former, as also a weary Nepal, had hoped that the Maoists would get sufficient number of seats as not to be so disheartened as to renew the insurgency and continue in a multi-party democratic framework. So far, the exercise had been about curtailing the powers of the king, ending the insurgency and weaning the Maoists into open, electoral democracy. These expectations received a jolt with the Maoists receiving 30 per cent of the votes, far ahead of the two major parties, the Nepali Congress and the UML (Unified Marxist Leninist), and exactly 50 per cent of the seats to which direct elections were held. Ironically, the Maoists had been keen on a mixed electoral system under which some seats would come under proportional representation, as they were unsure of faring well in direct contests with the established political parties. If all seats had been decided on the basis of direct elections, as had been the norm in Nepal and as is prevalent in the rest of South Asia, the Maoists may well have been in a position to form a government on their own.

The election results carried stark messages for the mainstream parties. Many of their leaders were comprehensively defeated and their presumed hold on the electorate was clearly in serious jeopardy. The Maoists had proved to be a serious challenge to politics as known till then. The atmosphere of co-operation and coordination seen after *jana andolan II* was clouded by concern and suspicion, which continues. But if the mainstream parties reeled from the shock results of the elections, the Maoists did not engender confidence by what was seen as frequent contradictions in their approach to multi-party democracy.

Of the issues, which confront the nation and divide opinions today, the future of federalism is the most complex. It is not a simple question of fashioning smaller administrative units for better governance. The urge for federalism represents a long standing desire of hitherto marginalized communities to be accorded the recognition due to them. This, in turn, has led to the demand for ethnic federalism where ethnic groups would have a decisive say in areas where they have a majority. There is no geographical area within Nepal where any group can claim a substantive majority. This can be a political nightmare with fears of ethnic strife in areas to be demarcated. The fundamental issue of addressing hitherto ignored and entirely justified pleas from ethnic minorities is lost in the debate on federalism. And an additional, forceful, element of this debate is the demand of the *madhesis* to be freed from the total administrative control of a central government which has, in the past, identified Nepal with its hills and looked on them as less than equal citizens.

India often looms large in the Nepali political discourse. Over the past many decades, India has been associated with political developments in Nepal. Nepali political leaders had supported India's struggle for independence and served time in British jails. Movements against the Rana regime in the 40s and 50s had found support and sanctuary in India. Nepali Congress had carried out agitation against *panchayati raj* from Indian soil. The *jana andolan* of 1990 had the open support of many senior Indian politicians. The 12 point agreement of November, 2005, between mainstream political parties and the Maoists was concluded in Delhi with Indian facilitation. The examples could be multiplied.

India is often charged with an intrusive approach in Nepal's internal politics. Understandably, the charges stem from those, who may be at the losing end of a political development. What is seldom acknowledged is that almost without exception, Nepali politicians have seemed anxious to gather Indian support for their own programmes and sought advice. Even if such advice were to be entirely objective, clearly it would not please all. One may recall that many years ago, the then Nepali foreign minister, eminent scholar and diplomat, Rishikesh Shaha had sought a meeting with Jawaharlal Nehru to seek his advice. Nehru had responded that he was always welcome. However, he said, whenever India responded to such requests, it would subsequently be described as interference. In this respect, little seems to have changed. With the multiple changes taking place in Nepal, both countries need to look at this aspect of the relationship, so that there are no misgivings among two sovereign nations.

Indo-Nepal relations do not fall under the usual paradigm of inter-state relations. The multiplicity of points of contact and interaction, cultural connectivities, legacies of history and common mythology, and the compulsions of geography have contributed to a complex relationship where conventional models simply do not apply. There is an inner stability in the relationship even as it remains, in some ways, amorphous and intangible. The stability is provided by a degree of recognition by both governments and peoples that there is mutual advantage in a framework of co-operation. There are no 'issues' between Nepal and India that are not capable of resolution by informed discourse and neither, fortunately, carries the kind of negative historical baggage as may be seen in some other South Asian relationships.

But propinquity can carry its own pitfalls. The connectivities between India and Nepal are so many that it is tempting to assume that we know enough of each other and there is no need to explore further or enhance our mutual understanding. This would be particularly true of India today as it must assess and understand the seminal changes that are underway in Nepal. The prism through which India views Nepal now needs careful adjustment.

Nepal has always been an important element in India's foreign policy considerations. This is seen even in the earliest days in Jawaharlal Nehru's many letters and notes, even pre-dating independence, which display his abiding concern for democracy in Nepal and the welfare of its people. It is instructive to recall that in an exchange in parliament, Nehru did not consider opposition to the then Rana regime to be treasonous simply because they came from communists.

There is a misperception that the 1950 treaty defines Indo-Nepal relations. It may be more appropriate to assess that it was the underlying quality of Indo-Nepal relations that made the treaty possible. The elements of the treaty related to security have long been consigned to oblivion, even if they had an urgency at the time for both India and Nepal following the Chinese occupation of Tibet. The clauses of the treaty relating to the import of arms and preferential treatment to Indian investors have gradually withered away. A significant element of the treaty was the mutual grant of 'national treatment' to the citizens of the two countries (though in the case of Nepal, this was to be accorded at a future date when considered appropriate). Even as elements of the treaty have fallen into disuse with the passage of time, according national treatment remains a crucial factor. India has stated that it is open to all three options with regard to the future of the treaty, namely, continuation in the present form, renegotiation and termination. The last course may cause intractable legal problems with regard to the large numbers of Nepali citizens in India and Indian citizens in Nepal.

There are many agreements and bilateral arrangements between India and Nepal that are not in the purview of the 1950 treaty, including the recruitment of Gorkhas in the Indian army, on river waters and on currency. Some of these also go beyond the usual norm in bilateral relations. Several, including the 1950 Treaty have periodically come in for criticism in Nepal. As Nepal transforms into a more self assured democracy, it would be important for both the countries to look closely at existing agreements to see if they should need to be recast. It is possible that they are largely to the benefit of Nepal, but since a range of political parties have questioned their utility, or their origins, from time to time, a transparent discussion, also involving civil society, may be useful. In any fresh agreements, each would have to look at their nation's interests with a sense of sovereign responsibility.

Presently, Nepal is trying to come to grips with a host of national questions that have emerged or erupted in the past decade. The resolution of many critical issues would not be achieved without a degree of national consensus. Even in the unlikely event of a political party winning a majority in the elections (presently scheduled for November, 2013), majority alone would not deliver long-term answers. There is no longer underlying fear of the guns of the Maoist cadres (even if a few may like to think on those lines) and it is now possible for all the actors on the political scene to act together for the larger national good. There are impediments to this happy conclusion. If the aim of politics is political power, which is indeed a *sine qua non*, then it may follow that all opposition must be downgraded. Additionally, there is the question of distrust. Not only the distrust claimed by political parties to justify their narrow and exclusive political agendas, but the genuine distrust of the hitherto dispossessed, who have seen past promises come to nought and would now like iron-clad guarantees for the future. But if such differences are not uncommon in societies, there also comes a time in the life of a society when the essence of concern for the nation's future must lead to workable solutions, which are fair to all stakeholders. The days of feudalism, where benefits accrued to a select coterie, are over in Nepal. But this should not be replaced by a free for all, or create a host of new contradictions and injustices to replace the old. So far, despite stumbles, the Nepali political classes have belied the doomsayers and one can only hope that they can weave the many strands of the nation into a lasting and rich fabric.

India and Nepal are two neighbouring countries. The nature of their relationship is unique. No other country is so directly affected by internal political developments in Nepal as is India. Besides the millions of migrant Nepali workers in India, it is to India that large numbers fled during the Maoist insurgency. And it is to India that successive Nepali generations have looked as they fought against undemocratic regimes in their country. It is the waters from the Nepal Himalaya that contribute significantly to the flows of the Ganga. And Nepal lies across the flat Gangetic delta with security implications that need no elaboration. The unity of the Nepali state and the welfare of all its citizens will be of concern to India. Even as India may look with concern at any political instability in Nepal, it cannot directly influence developments. But as Nepal goes through the difficult process of transformation, India's co-operation and assistance to the extent desired by the government and the people must be forthcoming.

1
The End of a Royal Line

Shortly after 11 pm on June 1, 2001, one of my officers called to say that there were reports of shooting in Narayanhiti royal palace. Details were still not confirmed, but it was feared that King Birendra may have been shot. It was not clear at the time as to who was responsible. A little later, the assassination of the king and queen and several members of the family was confirmed. I informed Meera Shankar, the joint secretary in charge of the Nepal division in the Ministry of External Affairs, requesting her to pass on the information to the prime minister's office. I also spoke to Shumsher Sherif in the office of the President of India. The rest of the night was spent standing by the telephones, which rang incessantly. By about 3 am, the news had spread across Kathmandu. An agitated member of the Indian community, who had fresh memories of the Hrithik Roshan riots of the previous December, called to ask if the Indian community could be sheltered in the Embassy, if any mass agitation following the assassination was directed against the community. I assured him that, if necessary, such shelter would be provided. In the early hours I heard a helicopter in the direction of Narayanhiti, which is not far from the Indian ambassador's residence. This would have been the king's younger brother Gyanendra returning in haste from Pokhara.

The next day was spent largely in communicating with Delhi, which was anxious to send a very senior person to represent India at the funeral of the late king. Given the several possible ramifications and immediate reactions to the assassination, I was not anxious for a high level Indian representation at the funeral as law and order clearly could not be assured. But Delhi was insistent. I could get no response from the Nepali political or civilian establishment, all pleading that the decision would lie with the palace. Eventually, shortly after mid-day, a tearful press secretary at the palace told me that while they were deeply grateful for India's sympathy and offer to be represented, the ground situation was so fragile that foreign guests simply could not be invited. Subsequent events in the evening, when even the Nepali prime minister's car in the cortege was targeted, bore out the validity of the concerns.

If Nepal was in a state of shock and grief after the royal massacre, it did not help matters that there was no direction to the government's efforts to stabilize emotions. While curfew was imposed in the face and fear of public violence, the facts remained shrouded. And nothing explains this more vividly than the declaration of crown prince Dipendra as the new king, when all, who should have known, knew that he was the sole perpetrator. Fortunately for all, Dipendra, who had suffered a gunshot wound in the head, succumbed to his injury three days later. It was then possible to pick up the pieces.

Given the government's unconvincing reaction to and explanation of the events, it was inevitable that there should be a spate of rumours and accusations, even if not always loudly announced. The intention of the palace was to be certain with regard to succession, but the secrecy and the haste of the cremations, the black-out on news only fuelled dire speculations. The chief victim of this was Gyanendra, crowned king in the sober and grief laden morning of June 4 after Dipendra expired. Even as he was accepted as king, suspicions remained that as the chief and final beneficiary of the massacre, he must have planned it, also noting that his son, Paras, had been left unharmed by Dipendra (his wife Komal was shot, but survived). None was spared the needle of suspicion. Prime Minister GP Koirala was seen as a conspirator trying to avoid charges of corruption, while the Maoists were obvious suspects. Inevitably, involvement of India was hinted, while the Maoist leadership saw a wide conspiracy to target Birendra as he was a nationalist.

The Maoists had maintained contacts with Birendra even as the insurgency was waged after 1996. Following the palace massacre, fulsome tributes were paid by Baburam Bhattarai and Prachanda.

Bhattarai wrote a remarkable letter to Kantipur, acknowledging past links with Birendra and suggesting foreign conspiracies in his assassination, implicating India for trying to 'Sikkimise' Nepal and also calling on the army to join the patriotic forces. Gyanendra was directly accused of complicity *(See at the end of the chapter)*. For future historians, Baburam Bhattarai's letter is also important as the first open declaration of republican intentions. Ten years later, Bhattarai was to stand by his suspicions, "I stick by what I said about the massacre ten years ago. Without a well planned political conspiracy, the whole family of King Birendra could not have been wiped out while Gyanendra's family remained unharmed," he said in an interview with reporters of the Nepali Times *(Kurakani, Hindustan Times)*. In an interview with Neelesh Mishra, Prachanda said, "In our opinion, King Birendra considered, from a feudal nationalistic point of view, the Maoist movement as a patriotic movement. It is further justified by his reluctance to use the army against the Maoist movement, and stress on granting amnesty to the Maoists and resolving the issue through talks. About one month before the murder, he had sent a message of his will to meet us through his youngest brother Dhirendra Shah, who was also murdered with him. We had a direct meeting with Dhirendra Shah only. A plan to hold talks directly with the late King Birendra was being worked out but it could not materialize due to his murder.... According to our study, King Birendra held a patriotic and anti-Indian expansionism stand and politically, he was comparatively a liberal feudal." He could, therefore, be expected to play the role of a Norodom Sihanouk in Nepal *(Neelesh Mishra, End of the Line: The Story of the Killing of the Royals in Nepal, 2001)*.

The reactions of Baburam Bhattarai and Prachanda, with their encomiums to Birendra, could well have been motivated by a desire to spread disrespect for the continued institution of the monarchy and the establishment as whole. Their conclusions may have been ideologically driven, with limited regard for accepting the fact of a demented prince indulging in an orgy of murder and mayhem. What stands out, and is of historical importance, however, is the public admission of the efforts to bring together the far right and the far left in the late 90s. It may not exonerate the political parties for their failure to deliver on people's expectations, but it does at least partially explain the handicap of a silently manipulative palace under whose aura they had to function.

In this context, Baburam's letter acquires significance. Bhattarai and Prachanda confirmed what had been long suspected. At a future date, perhaps, details would emerge of the steps contemplated to destabilize the democratic centre. This was a compact that Gyanendra was to break to his cost, as he targeted democracy on his own.

After his accession, King Gyanendra established a three-member commission to investigate the killing, but as Madhav Kumar Nepal declined to participate on the plea of not being authorized by his party, the commission was left with two persons. The commission then comprised of Chief Justice K.P. Upadhyaya and the speaker of the House of Representatives, T. Ranabat. In its report, which was published in mid-June, it confirmed that Prince Dipendra was responsible for the killings and that time, he was under the influence of drugs and alcohol. According to an official statement, the killings were caused by "an accidental discharge of automatic weapons". The Enquiry Commission confirmed that Dipendra had ingested some whisky (the Famous Grouse brand) and smoked cigarettes with some brown particles (hashish). Dipendra was either inebriated or acting so, and was escorted to his bed chamber upstairs. A while later, he descended carrying three automatic rifles and the mayhem started (The term used to describe the discharge of weapons in the original Nepali report was *'akasmik'*, which translates into 'sudden' and not 'accidental', as inaccurately conveyed in the English version).

The decimation of the royal house of what till recently was considered a Shangrila was understandable fuel for speculation. The handling of the crisis added further scope for rumour mongering. Contrary to apprehensions, street violence soon abated. Large numbers of men shaved their heads in the traditional mark of mourning. The coronation of Gyanendra was accepted without any visible demur, though in the minds of some, Birendra remained the last king of Nepal.

In terms of basic attitudes to the philosophy of governance, Birendra was not greatly different from his father Mahendra, who had dismissed the parliament and brought in *panchayati raj,* or his brother Gyanendra, who tried to rule directly. But even if Birendra was not unwilling to see the failure of the democratic experiment, wrested from him in 1990, he had the wisdom to bow before the will of the people or, at least, not to be seen to be obstructive and remained in the people's affections as a people's king. The grief at his passing was genuine.

Of the several milestones, which the history of Nepal has recorded in the past decade or so, the palace massacre of June 1, 2001, may have had the most far reaching consequences. It may or may not have been possible to arrive at a negotiated end to the insurgency within the existing framework and, if the Bhattarai-Prachanda account is to be believed, Birendra may have emerged as a Sihanouk. But Gyanendra was to go on to ensure the end of monarchy itself. The issues of recognition of the rights of minorities and ethnic groups had been simmering for long. The resolution of these was now to be coupled with the definition of the state itself. For over two hundred years, the king had been projected, and accepted as the symbol of Nepal. *L'état, c'est moi* applied more to Nepal than the France of Louis XIV.

A fresh definition of Nepali nationhood would now be required. An entirely new era had emerged.

(BABURAM BHATTARAI'S OPEN LETTER)

Kantipur, June 6

Let's Give No Legitimacy to the Beneficiaries of the New Kot Massacre.

Baburam Bhattarai

There was another Kot massacre in Nepal's history on June 1st, 2001. Since the people are yet to get the facts of the tragedy, which killed King Birendra and other members of the Nepali royal family, it is evident that people everywhere are speculating and weighing conspiracy theories. As the saying goes, "paap-dhuri bata karaucha" [The sin shouts from the roof of the sinner's house], we will one day know the truth. No one is ready to believe the propaganda, which is being spread by the government and it's foreign masters, especially since the way in which this tragedy is being explained—either the love affair or the accidental explosion theory—gives strong reasons to believe that the government itself is behind this tragedy. But this will only strengthen the just claim of the Nepali people to know the truth. So, a coalition between the nationalists and the people's forces (NCP-Maoist) to unveil the real villains of the tragedy is what history demands from us at this particular moment of time.

The Reactionary world view presents any historic incident as a mere accident and tries to put the blame on some particular person. And it also tries to hide the core reality of the incident and only focuses on what is seen at the surface level. Analyzed from this angle, the recent tragedy in Nepal might be made to appear to be about a love affair and the government and its foreign masters' media are busily presenting this view. Further, another explanation that the gun exploded by itself and killed the key persons of the royal household was put out by the prime beneficiaries of the tragedy—perhaps motivated by the fear of what the survivors of the tragedy will say later. Undoubtedly, many historic events are mere accidents, and someone's unconscious urges or momentary craziness could also play an important part. However, these exceptions have to correspond to a series of believable events, which simply is not the case in the recent tragedy. A future king might give up his chance to sit on the throne to be with the girl he loves, but we cannot be asked to believe that he would physically eliminate his entire family and then commit suicide for love. Moreover, to say that an automatic gun itself entered a highly secured room and killed the King and his immediate family, while leaving the members of the new King's immediate family uninjured, is an insult to the thinking power of every being that breathes—let alone science and logic. We have heard of many scientific innovations, but if anyone has ever invented such a weapon, is he not entitled to the throne of not only the Narayanhiti Royal Palace but also of the Delhi Palace and the White House?

On the contrary, the Progressive materialist and dialectical world view explains any given incident as part of the pattern of the flow of life and the events taking place around the world. And any incident is seen as a product resulting from the intertwining of historical necessity and accident. Looked at from this angle, in any given incident, the underlying structures of social life play an important role, and the players who are seen associated with it from outside or at the surface level are but accidental. This makes it imperative for us to look at the massacre which took place in the Narayanhiti royal palace vis-a-vis the class struggle and people's revolution taking places in Nepal and elsewhere in the world.

The centralized kingdom of Nepal, established under the leadership of King Prithvi Narayan Shah some 215 years ago, was in a rather bleak state in 2058 [2001]. It was — and it is — impossible to deal with the situation in a traditional way and under the old class rule. Plus, Nepal's geopolitical situation and the changing power dynamics in the world and South Asia are making it hard to preserve Nepal's national unity and sovereignty in the same old traditional way. What we have to understand here is that Nepal was always under the influence of British imperialism from the time of the Sugauli treaty [1816], and later came under the direct influence of Indian expansionism. Nepal has witnessed the direct influence of expansionist and imperialist powers ever since the death of the nationalist Bhimsen Thapa [1839] through the rise of the British Dog (description courtesy of Karl Marx) Jung Bahadur after the Kot massacre, and in each successive political change. It shouldn't be very hard for Nepali nationalists to understand the new Kot massacre as a continuation of the same pattern of "influence."

Why was King Birendra and his family murdered at this particular moment? What was his crime in the eyes of the expansionist and imperialist powers? Whatever your political ideology might be, one thing every honest Nepali nationalist has to agree with is this: King Birendra's liberal political ideology and his patriotism were seen as his weakness and had become a crime in the eyes of the expansionist and imperialist powers. During the one-sided Indian economic embargo and revolution of 1990, instead of surrendering himself to the expansionist powers, he surrendered to his people. This did not make the expansionist forces happy. Later, his unwillingness to mobilize the army—which has a tradition of loyalty towards the King—to curb the People's Revolution taking place under the leadership of Nepal Communist Party (Maoist) became his biggest crime in the eyes of the imperialist and expansionist powers. Some Marxist pundits, based on this, called us a pro-monarchy party, and we can now say that we—NCP (Maoist) and King Birendra—had similar views on many national issues and this had created in fact an informal alliance between us. Obviously, this scared the imperialist powers and their cronies. In the context of a deteriorating Sino-US relationship and a growing strategic alliance between India and the US, the King who appeared soft on us—the Maoists—and China had become an irritation to the American Imperialists and especially to the Indian expansionists.

India's dream of annexing Nepal like Sikkim had to be amended and instead they had to make Nepal a Bhutan first, before making it another Sikkim. After CIA (and the recently opened FBI branch in Delhi) approval, RAW (Research and Analysis Wing) [the Indian covert intelligence and operations agency] came up with a grand master plan to annex Nepal. Just like the cunning fox of folk-lore who stole the chickens by falsely shouting that an eagle was arriving, RAW too created a fake tale about the ISI (Inter Service Intelligence) [the Pakistani covert intelligence and operations agency] being active in Nepal and having penetrated the Palace. [The next few sentences, which refer to the 1964 Bhutan events, suggest a direct involvement of the new royal family in the June 1st slaughter] They even chose a Jigme Sigme for the Bhutanization of Nepal. And it is through that Jigme Sigme that the massacre was carried out. There shouldn't be any doubt that RAW, which had already found their Lendup Dorje in Girija [the current pro-Indian Nepali Congress Prime Minister], aligned the new Jigme Sigme with their Lendup Dorje for the Bhutanization of Nepal, with a goal of eventual Sikkimization of Nepal.

What's the new responsibility of every Nepali nationalist in this situation? A press release issued by our Party secretary, Comrade

Prachanda has already appealed to the nationalist forces to develop a new analysis and form a new unity on a new basis and move forward together. Emphasizing that appeal, we request that every nationalist and leftist force speed up their thinking and actions to the same fast rate at which these incidents have been happening. In this historic moment, one small mistake by us can bring calamities to the nation and its people, whereas our one wise step can lead Nepal and Nepalis into the 21st century proud of their country and themselves. Our first wise step will be to identify the grand design behind this new Kot massacre and unveil the culprits. We must also deny legitimacy to the beneficiaries of this new Kot massacre, because this is 2001 not 1846, and in this gap, not only an enormous amount of water has flowed in the Koshi, Karnali and Gandaki rivers, but also an enormous amount of blood has flowed. Despite the differences on many issues, an important contribution of the Shah Kings (from Prithvi Narayan Shah to King Birendra) has been to preserve Nepali independence and sovereign status from the hands of British imperialism and later from Indian expansionism. But, now, if any Shah dreams of establishing a new Rana rule by staging a Kot massacre with the help of expansionists, then there is no question of giving legitimacy to his rule by the Nepali people. The contribution made by kings—from Prithvi Narayan Shah to King Birendra—will be valued highly by the Nepali people for ages, but at any cost they will not accept the new Jigme Sigme, who has come to power by staging a Kot massacre. In this context, the RNA (Royal Nepali Army), whose main duty is to serve the King and the country, should re-assess their role after their failure to save the King. It is time for the army to think of new ways to save the country. We sincerely request that the army join hands with the patriots born in small huts across Nepal, instead of joining hands with the puppet of expansionist forces in the palace. The country is in crisis, and it is very important for all the nationalist forces to come together....sabailai chetana bhaya—may everyone understand this.

2
Political Developments 1990-2001

1990 had heralded a new beginning for the politics and the state of Nepal. The first people's movement was born in February 1990 under the unprecedented joint leadership of the Nepali Congress and seven communist parties, which came together as the United Left Front (ULF). As the movement progressed, it drew large swathes of Nepali society, including marginalized groups, professional classes and trade unions, into a broad alliance with the pro-democracy political parties, challenging the *panchayat's* grip.

The *jana andolan* brought to an end the *panchayati raj* instituted by king Mahendra three decades earlier. There was support from political elements in India, notably Chandra Shekhar, who was later briefly to be the Indian prime minister. Birendra suppressed his emotions and wisely refrained from a bloody confrontation with his people.

The movement resulted in what was interpreted as the end of absolute monarchy and the establishment of a multi-party parliamentary form of government under a constitutional monarchy. The constitution that emerged, however, was one negotiated by a few and not the product of a constituent assembly for which the people had already waited forty years. There was still among many of the actors of the day inherent awe and respect for the monarchy and this was reflected in the constitution. While "the sovereignty of Nepal is vested in the Nepalese people", the king was not only the "symbol of Nepalese nationality", but also "the unity of the Nepalese people". By implication, a Nepal without a king was a rudderless entity. He was, furthermore, an "adherent of Aryan culture". This emphasis underlines the differences with those not claiming Aryan descent which, in a way, is reflected in the bitter debate on federalism today. Article 23 (3) expected the king to "preserve and protect this Constitution by keeping in view the best interests and welfare of the people of Nepal", a provision to be liberally interpreted by Gyanendra fifteen years later to effect his royal coup. He was to "operate and use the Royal Nepal Army on the recommendation of the National Defence Council". In reality, the NDC, which never functioned, was by passed, and at a critical moment in 2001, the army chief had no hesitation in letting it be known that the king's wishes were paramount.

Birendra believed in the absolute powers of the monarchy. As quoted by Rishikesh Shaha, he believed that "... the King embodies the collective identity of the people and, as desired by the people, it is he who grants and amends the constitution" *(Rishikesh Shaha, Nepali Politics, Retrospect and Prospect, Oxford University Press, 1978).* But even if he had agreed to step back from direct confrontation with the people and political parties in 1990, Birendra and the palace were happy to see, if not encourage, political dissensions. As Kanak Mani Dixit puts it, though remembered as a lenient king, he (Birendra) ruled for two decades as an autocrat and after 1990 tried to "constantly access power at the cost of elected governments" *(Kanak Mani Dixit, Peace Politics of Nepal, Himal Books, 2011).*

Besides the relationship with the palace, whose outlines had not been spelt out or acknowledged by either side, the political parties did not distinguish themselves with a series of inter and intra-party differences, leading to frequent changes in government. The challenges before the newly empowered political parties were formidable. A nation imbued with attitudes of *chakari,* or sychophancy, to feudal overlords had to be weaned into assurance. Institutions, which had depended for their survival on the palace, had to be given new independent identities. Democracy had been a long time coming to Nepal and it had to be guided and nurtured. Economic deprivation in the neglected countryside had to be redressed and, not the least, the issues of identity, which had simmered unattended for long, had to be addressed. The latter would not receive sufficient attention and would provide the building blocks for the Maoist insurgency in the years to come.

The account of politics in the decade following the *jana andolan* is a tedious tale of personality based politics and changes of affiliation by all the political parties in their quest for power. The grand old party of Nepal, the Nepali Congress, which had been in the forefront of all movements for five decades for the establishment of the rights of the people, found itself crippled by the personality conflicts at the top. G.P. Koirala and K.P. Bhattarai each tried to ensure that the other would not be allowed to function either within the party or as the head of the government. The principled votary of democracy and the leading light of the *jana andolan,* Ganesh Man Singh was ignored by those thirsting for power. The frequent changes in government and leadership — ten changes in prime minister from 1990-2001, some in repeat appearances — could not be conducive to sustained governance. As Dixit points out, "… The problem of the 1990 constitution was not with regard to content but implementation. It was a democratic constitution which confirmed for the first time that sovereignty lay in the people. But even as it ushered Nepal into the modern era, the neophyte political parties showed their all too obvious weaknesses in terms of mal-governance, corruption and inter-party bickering *(Dixit: Ibid)*.

It was also a period when both the major parties, the NC and the UML, were not averse to seeking the intervention of the palace to gain their own ends, while the palace was only too pleased to see the parties discredit themselves. There is near unanimity among analysts of the time that the political parties contributed to the palace regaining the influence lost in 1990 and being able to project itself as the only stable institution in Nepal. Additionally, the NC had no hesitation in welcoming within its fold former adherents of the *panchayati raj* now seeking greener pastures, to the obvious dismay and resentment of its long term supporters and cadres, besides creating rifts with the UML. Both the parties politicized appointments to government positions, more in their pursuit of benefits rather than for the implementation of policies. The disbursement of patronage instead of consolidating support at the grassroots and commitment to ideology would exact a heavy price from both the Nepali Congress and the UML in the years to come.

Understandably, the Nepali Congress emerged as the leading party after 1990 and won a majority in the first elections held in 1991. The advantage was soon lost and it was to be relegated to the second position in the 1994 elections. In the game of musical chairs, unstable coalition governments soon became the norm. There were five prime ministers heading seven governments in the period from 1994 till the dissolution of the House in 1999. An eminent scholar reviews the politics of the period:

"The personalities of the Congress troika leaders, which had been used by almost all Congress candidates in attracting the voters in the 1991 parliamentary elections, figured low in the party's campaign strategy in the 1994 and 1999 elections. Thus, the NC's capacity to attract the masses through its ideology and its leaders decreased after the first general election of 1991 as the NC relied increasingly on the other main method of party building, which was through patronage...... With the objective of being re-elected, Congress parliamentarians and ministers had strived to provide services to the power-brokers in their own electoral constituencies. In this regard, almost each of the Congress leaders, MPs and ministers had records of providing jobs and other favours to several hundred persons during the three and half years rule of the Congress government

"…. Once the UML got to power, it bluntly manipulated the state resources for the purpose of patronage. The formation of the Commission for Landless at the Central and the Local levels was another lucrative avenue for party clients. The transformation of the party loyalists to the post of Local Development Officer (LBO) with the power of dispending funds to the BYVY programme and the provision of all party committee at the Village Development Committee level to spend such funds was one of the several instances, which suggested the UML government used development resources to satisfy its various clients, although the reports had not come out openly" *(Krishna Hachhethu, Political Parties and the State, 2003).*

Halfway through the decade, the Maoists made an emphatic entry on the political scene. The history of communist parties in Nepal had been chequered. Formed in Calcutta in 1949, already by the mid-50s, an influential section of it had been cajoled by the palace to support the monarchy. A distinguished former diplomat told me that he had asked Mahendra in the early 60s if the king did not find any contradiction, or danger, in supporting communists who, at the time, were beneficiaries of government largesse. Mahendra had replied that this was necessary due to the compulsions of the time and was not a policy that would be sustained. Obviously, the palace considered the communists an useful foil against the Nepali Congress with its wide reach and progressive pro-people agenda.

The violent Jhapa movement from 1974, where class enemies were beheaded, took its inspiration from Naxalbari across the border and the Chinese Cultural Revolution. The movement mellowed gradually and eventually transmuted into the Communist Party of Nepal (United Marxist Leninist). As an interesting, but possibly illuminating aside, a Nepali friend pointed out that the Nepali *topi* worn by the Nepali Congress is black in colour, while the UML sports the colourful 'dhaka' *topi* as favoured by the palace. Separately, a radical communist movement grew in western Nepal.

Meanwhile, a great deal of ideological churning had been taking place among the radical communists, with groups forming and re-forming. While tactics differed, there was broad agreement that existing systems of representation and governance would have to be recast in the *naulo janabad,* the new people's democracy. Eventually, Baburam Bhattarai, the uncompromising ideologue, was to join Prachanda and they would provide the leadership to the Maoist insurgency as it evolved. The participation of the radicals in the elections in 1991 was avowedly tactical and the ultimate goals remained consistent.

A significant section of the government looked at the movement of radical communists as entirely a law and order problem, with little effort to either appreciate, let alone address, the aspirations of the people following the restoration of democracy. Operation Romeo was launched in November, 1995, in mid-western Nepal. Innocent villagers were frequently targeted and there were serious human rights violations. This, in turn, would result in greater sympathy for the radicals. The subsequent Kilo Serra operations had similar consequences and were to strengthen the insurgency.

In what was to become a point of reference in the history of Nepal, Baburam Bhattarai submitted a 40-point demand to the prime minister on February 4, 1996 with a deadline of two weeks. As the letter concluded, "If there are no positive indications towards this from the government by 17 February, 1996, we would like to inform you that we will be forced to adopt the path of armed struggle against the existing state power."

Many of the 40 points would seem unexceptionable in a democratic society concerned with freedom and the welfare of its citizens. Some struck at the existing structure of state and society. India came in for special mention. Ideally, the issues raised could have been discussed. But, obviously, the Maoists wanted the 'charter' of the 40 points for propaganda purposes, while the government would continue to look at the radicals as a law and order nuisance. Neither, with entirely different calculations, was anxious to come to a negotiated settlement. Subsequent half-hearted efforts to negotiate through intermediaries could never progress as there was neither a sense of urgency nor any defined position maintained. The Maoist insurgency was now formally on its way.

In a remarkable display of short-sightedness, the major political parties thought they could garner political benefits from the insurgency. The Nepali Congress expected that the Maoists would detract from the support base of their major political opponents, the UML. The latter, meanwhile, were pleased that the initial acts of intimidation and violence of the Maoists were directed at the NC. Not insignificantly, the Maoists did not target those with proximity to the palace. During these years, G.P. Koirala was more inflexible, while K.P. Bhattarai showed a greater will to find negotiated solutions. He was to appoint Sher Bahadur Deuba to try and find a way out. It was no secret at the time that Deuba found but scant support from within his party for his efforts. In July 2001, days before he was to assume the office of prime minister once again, Deuba had told me that he considered his discussions with the Maoists to have been fruitful and that the answer did not lie in a military solution, but in trying to address genuine demands.

While the political parties continued with their uncoordinated approach to the insurgency, the palace was happy at their discomfiture. While there was, as yet, no direct proof, there was inferential evidence that the palace and the Maoists were in contact. This was not surprising as extremes of left and right have a common interest in degrading a democratic centre as represented, in this case, by the NC and the UML. While paying fulsome tributes to Birendra after his assassination, both Baburam Bhattarai and Prachanda were to admit that they had been in touch with him.

The insurgency in the countryside and the progressively increasing hold of the Maoists had left Kathmandu unperturbed. Reality was brought home when, in July 2001, even as the nation was recovering from the shock of the palace massacre, the Maoists simultaneously attacked a large number of police outposts in the west, killing many and holding many hostage. Prime Minister Koirala, also holding the defence portfolio, wanted the Royal Nepal Army to act instantly, but King Gyanendra would not comply and the Chief of the Army Staff made it plain that no movement would take place without royal instructions. Responding to charges of elected governments not taking sufficient measures to contain the Maoists, Koirala was to comment bitterly that when Maoist hold on the countryside was limited, "We repeatedly told His Majesty to use the military against the Maoists, failing which they could spread. But the military was reluctant to go and the king was hesitant to move. How can the royal palace now blame the political parties for its own actions?" Koirala resigned, and was succeeded by Sher Bahadur Deuba, who commenced negotiations with the Maoists. Maoist demands were the abolition of the monarchy, formation of an interim government and elections to a constituent assembly, with emphasis on the last. The negotiations continued desultorily until November, 2001, when the Maoist carried out a spectacular attack on an army camp, simultaneously destroying government installations in Dang and Syangja. This was the first attack on the RNA by the Maoists in their five years of operations. An emergency was declared on November 26 and the Royal Nepal Army began their offensive against the Maoists. A new phase in the insurgency and the politics of Nepal had commenced.

The *jana andolan* of 1990 had swept away the *panchayati raj* and brought in multi-party democracy to Nepal, introducing the nation belatedly to the 20th century. From the definition of the citizen as "having common aspirations and united by the common bond of allegiance to the Crown" of the 1962 constitution, the 1990 constitution proudly declaimed, "WHEREAS, We are convinced that the source of sovereign authority of the independent and sovereign Nepal is inherent in the people, and, therefore, We have, from time to time, made known our desire to conduct the government of the country in consonance with the popular will." But the main actors had been steeped in a tradition of *chakari* and awe of the palace. Hence, the ambiguous clauses, which were to be later misused by Gyanendra. The challenges before the new political actors were formidable. Ingrained feudal attitudes among both the rulers and the ruled had to be chiselled away. A wholly fresh ethos of governance and response to simmering resentments and aspirations had to evolve. These were not forthcoming, even as the nation saw a sorry display of unprincipled politics in the pursuit of power. The role of the palace was not positive, even as the political parties curried favours and permitted the palace to exercise influences that were quite outside the intended purview of the constitution.

The political discourse in Nepal, then as now, is about politics, with not much attention paid to other developments that take place. Even though expectations were clearly not fulfilled, it may be appropriate in balance to also refer to some positive aspects of this lost decade as seen by Kanak Mani Dixit, "True participatory development was absent for three decades and only began with the advent of multiparty democracy in 1990. In fact, almost all the tools and processes of civil society, from free media to developmental activism were developed after 1990 in the democratic era...... It was during these dozen years from 1990 to 2002, exactly half of which were disrupted by the Maoist insurgency, that the people learnt to challenge authority from the village level up……. For the first time, the districts got attention and power and representation became more than a token game in which feudal overlords appointed by Kathmandu ruled. …… assertions of ethnic identity built up steam, community forestry succeeded, local self government was put in place and genuine entrepreneurship began to take root in a business community long used to crony capitalism and contraband trade" *(Dixit: Ibid.)*.

Others may argue that feudal appointments were replaced by ones for political advantage and that some of the positive developments owed not so much to affirmative action by politicians, but to the Nepali people, particularly the middle classes and civil society, who had been awakened to fresh opportunities and challenges.

3
Political Developments 2001-2013

King Gyanendra was at the centre stage in Nepal in the early part of the last decade. Having been both crowned and dethroned five decades earlier, following his grandfather's flight from, and return to, Kathmandu, he once again found himself the king of Nepal in the most trying circumstances. Though the circumstances of his brother's assassination were clear, detractors and rumour mongers wondered if he was in some way responsible. Only many years later, in his farewell address after parliament had decreed an end to monarchy, did he dwell on it, "I and my family have been continuously defamed with ill intentions, which was saddening and still is. The accusations that were targeted against us were inhuman." But however unjust and unjustified the rumours, in the minds of many common Nepali, Birendra was their last king. It did not help that by both conviction and demeanour, Gyanendra believed in the right of the dynasty to rule, not merely reign. But the circumstances on the ground had changed since Mahendra's time, and he lacked Birendra's finesse.

The major challenge was, of course, the Maoist insurgency. It was five years old when Gyanendra ascended the throne and was becoming more assured, leaving its violent signature across the nation. Six months into his reign, they attacked the Royal Nepal Army, followed by the emergency. Even though the palace had kept discreet lines open to the Maoists, it was no longer possible now to continue to let the politicians take sole responsibility, and the army had to be actively involved in anti-insurgency operations. Events unfolded as they did, but it is clear that Gyanendra had decided early that he was the man who would be in control. Engaging and alert, he could carry on a lively conversation late into the night, never losing for a moment the essential thread of what he wanted to convey. Early in his reign, he would sit on a sofa at the same level as his visitor. In a few months, he reverted to Birendra's practice of a higher, more ornamental chair for himself as his sense of superiority grew. So, apparently, did his distance from ground realities. In the next few years, he would treat the political classes with increasingly open contempt, an error of judgement born of hubris, which was to lead, eventually, to the end of his dynasty.

As Maoist violence increased, Deuba dissolved the parliament in May, 2002. The extension of the emergency, which curtailed civil liberties and free expression, was becoming an increasingly contentious issue. The security situation in the country did not permit elections, which were to be held within six months of the dissolution of the House. On October 4, 2002, Gyanendra dismissed the Deuba government, claiming, "The greater good of Nepal and the Nepali people is our only goal" and charging Deuba with "incompetence" for not holding elections in time. Invoking articles 27(3) and 127 of the constitution, Gyanendra assumed executive powers, "As it will take some time to make new arrangements, we will exercise the executive powers of the Kingdom of Nepal until such arrangements are in place and we ourselves undertake the responsibility of governance in the country." Elections due for the following month, he said, would have to be deferred. From here to becoming the CEO of Nepal in February, 2005 would be a short step.

Even in this twilight zone where the gains of the *jana andolan* were visibly receding, Gyanendra found willing takers for the post of prime minister. Former prime ministers Lokendra Bahadur Chand, Surya Bahadur Thapa and Sher Bahadur Deuba served between October, 2002 and February, 2005, when the last was dismissed once again as Gyanendra took full personal charge. There had been no parliament, but political parties sent their representatives to the council of ministers. The Nepali Congress had held out.

As the game of musical chairs went on in Kathmandu, Nepal continued to bleed from the insurgency. Atrocities were committed by both the Maoists and the Royal Nepal Army. Faced with these twin threats, large numbers fled across the border to India. Even those who had agreed to serve in government felt the pressure of public opinion. The political situation of the time is captured by Prof. Lok Raj Baral, "In November 2003, reports claimed that senior CPN (UML) leaders Madhav Kumar Nepal met with key Maoists, Prachanda and Baburam Bhattarai in Lucknow, India. The meeting created tremendous pressure for Prime Minister Surya Bahadur Thapa, who reportedly got calls from his own party members to resign from the post of Prime Ministership in order to release the political pressure and to stop the trend towards a dialogue between the Maoists and the opposition parties" *(Lok Raj Baral, Nepal, History in South Asia, Routledge Publications, 2009).*

As the political and military stalemate continued, demonstrations became frequent and violent with students and citizenry with no overt party affiliations being involved, even as the Maoists carried out a week-long blockade of the Valley (August, 2004) and adopted urban targets. Discontent among the general population was rife. The groundwork for another *jana andolan* had been laid.

Events moved rapidly as Gyanendra decided that his personal rule alone could stem the tide of popular disaffection. On February 1, 2005, Gyanendra took over. Invoking Prithvinarayan Shah and the unification of Nepal, he asserted that "Nepal's independence, national unity and sovereignty are best safeguarded by the intimate relationship between the King and people," swore by multi-party democracy and promised elections when peace had been restored. His proclamation was a tirade against the failures of the political classes despite the opportunities offered to them. At one stroke, Gyanendra had cast pretensions aside and removed the shield which the political parties had hitherto provided him. Henceforth, by his own declaration, he and he alone would be answerable. Besides, he had ensured that of the three players on the political stage, two, namely the mainstream political parties and the Maoists, would now act in concert. With the concurrent imposition of emergency, many political leaders, including the recently dismissed Sher Bahadur Deuba, and civil society activists were arrested.

It was now time for the political parties to take stock and decide on future action. For some time, the Maoists had been seeking a safe landing on to the political scene. It was becoming clear that even if they controlled large tracts in the countryside, an outright military victory and capture of the state through military means was not possible. They had made significant gains in the countryside and their promises and programmes found resonance among ethnic minorities, *dalits* and women. It was time to try and cash in. Prachanda, the supremo and the most visible face of the movement, is said to have recommended an entente with the king, while Baburam preferred an understanding with the political parties. Prachanda's formula would have revived the incipient coalition between the extreme left and the extreme right which had been attempted in Birendra's reign (and which is again being considered by the breakaway, ideologically driven Vaidya faction with Gyanendra to protect 'nationalism'). For the mainstream parties, too, it was a moment of reckoning. Even though Gyanendra's intentions should have been clear after his assumption of executive powers in October, 2002, and the absence of a parliament, the political parties, with the exception of the Nepali Congress, had collaborated by participating in non-representative governments, thus giving them a gossamer cloak of respectability. This was at the cost of losing their own credibility among the people at a time when popular discontent was on the rise and no end visible to the insurgency. Regardless of what the king may affirm, he seemed the least likely candidate for bringing peace to Nepal. Gyanendra had surrounded himself with Mahendra's advisers from the *panchayat* era and the self-delusion of the parties in the preceding twilight years was no longer feasible. Darkness had descended with the royal coup of February, 2005 and the future seemed to portend a long night of a re-packaged *panchayati-raj.*

Reactions to the palace coup in India had been mixed. While civil society and media had been critical, there were extensive connectivities between the Nepali establishment and groups in India, who were not unwilling to look upon the coup as possibly not an unwelcome development, particularly if it helped in curbing the Maoists. The Rana-Shah ruling elite had close family bonds with erstwhile princely classes in India, while many looked benignly at the king of the only Hindu kingdom. To the concern that any seeming success for the Maoists would impact negatively on India's own violent left-wing movements, it was pointed out that it could be even more cogently argued that if the Nepali Maoists could be brought into the political mainstream, this would be a positive example for their Indian counterparts.

Essentially conservative and oriented towards status quo, the Indian establishment was not willing to take an unequivocal stand, even though India's reticence in attending the forthcoming SAARC Summit in Dhaka was partially influenced by the coup. The defence establishment in India, in particular, was supportive of the king's action citing its close relations with the Royal Nepal Army and made the specious argument that the feeling of the Gorkhas in the Indian army, presumed to be royalists, had to be taken into account. The transfer of military equipment from India was, however, stopped.

The king of Nepal and Prime Minister Manmohan Singh met in Jakarta in April while attending the Afro-Asian Summit. They agreed that it was necessary to restart the political process in Nepal at the earliest "and that this, in turn, would enable His Majesty's government to deal with the Maoist insurgency." Gyanendra's announcement that the Indians had agreed to resume arms supplies took the Indians by surprise and caused some brief international confusion as most countries had also banned arms supplies to Nepal. Arms supplies from India were not to resume. On return to Kathmandu, Gyanendra placed several political leaders under arrest, quite contrary to the political process the Indians had expected. As a leading Nepali journal commented wryly, the king had run rings round the Indians. The episode, however, helped persuade decision makers in Delhi that the king could not be relied upon. In the formulation of Indian policy at the time, key roles were played by the heads of the foreign and intelligence establishments, both personally acquainted with Nepal, and a perceptive ambassador in Kathmandu.

As the mainstream political parties and the Maoists came closer to an understanding, isolating the king, India was to play a facilitatory role as they attempted a roadmap for the future. Contacts had been established with the Maoists some years earlier as Nepal's political parties engaged with them, and these contacts were now intensified under political direction In an interaction in Delhi, Baburam Bhattarai asserted that around 2002, the Maoists realized the need for an understanding with the political parties and approached India for its good offices to this end (Round table organized by the Society for Policy Studies and the India International Centre on March 2, 2015. Prof. S.D. Muni had already written about this in some detail).

In seeking a solution to Nepal's political problems, three parallel crises had to be simultaneously addressed. There was the Maoist insurgency, the palace coup against democracy and the loss of credibility of the politicians. It was increasingly accepted that to achieve any movement towards the imperatives of peace, democracy and progressive programmes, it would be essential for the mainstream parties and the Maoists to arrive at a consensus. This could now be considered as some core changes in perceptions had taken place. The palace massacre of 2001 had shocked the Nepali people and partially de-mythified the institution of monarchy. Gyanendra's assumption of the continued sanctity of the monarchy in the Nepali mind was losing its validity as the country tried to grope for an identity beyond allegiance to the dynasty. The king's coup of 2005 hastened the process. The commonly accepted formula of the twin pillars of Nepal being constitutional monarchy and multi-party democracy was being eroded, with the will of the people increasingly being accepted as the sole pillar of Nepal's polity.

At the Chungbang meeting, the Maoists appeared amenable to entering into a collaborative effort to combat feudalism. In an interview to Bharat Bhushan of *The Telegraph*, Baburam admitted that the international situation made it difficult to sustain revolution in Nepal and that the restoration of democracy was a necessary intermediary step to the creation of a socialist state.

A broad based Indo-Nepal civil society dialogue in Delhi in August, 2005, concluded:

- On the home front, the Nepali people need to rejuvenate their political parties and bring them to the forefront of the struggle for the restoration of peace and democracy. This can only be done by challenging the king openly in the streets through peaceful protests and demonstrations by party activists and civil society actors.

- The Maoists cannot be left out of any final outcome and, therefore, a concerted effort must be made by the political parties to include them in a consultative process, leading to a peaceful resolution of the conflict through ideological change. They must be given a 'safe landing'.
- Ground realities of command and control, and the intertwining of the insurgency with local political economies must be taken into consideration and mechanisms must be devised for ensuring compliance and dismantling respectively.
- India's role should not be to give the king any more confidence, but to support the dialogue process between the political parties and the Maoists. The international community as a whole needs to exert greater pressure on the king to allow democratic change in Nepal.
- While third parties can create favourable conditions, the real agents of change have to be the people of Nepal. This includes political parties, the public, civil society, academics and the media *(Symposium held at the Centre for Policy Research on August 12, 2005).*

On November 22, 2005, the Seven Party Alliance concluded the 12 point agreement with the Maoists in Delhi. The seven parties represented 194 of the 205 seats of the last elected parliament of Nepal in 1999. The agreement was reached after days of intense negotiations. Delhi had provided the venue, but the conclusions were reached entirely by Nepali participants. At one point, Madhav Kumar Nepal of the UML had been categorical that the agreement would be reached by the Nepalis themselves without any directions from India. Girija Prasad Koirala, the tallest man in Nepal politics, remained consistently supportive. He had by now overcome and replaced his innate suspicion of communists with a distaste for Gyanendra and his policies.

The 12 Point understanding sought to end 'autocratic' monarchy (not very dissimilar to the demand in the 40 point demand of the Maoists of 1996) and, at this stage, there was no direct demand for the end of monarchy itself. Both sides agreed to introspect on their past mistakes and not to repeat them. It affirmed that "The seven agitating parties are fully committed to the fact that only by establishing absolute democracy through the restoration of the Parliament with the force of agitation, forming an all-party government with complete authority, holding elections to a constituent assembly through dialogue and understanding with the Maoists, can the existing conflict in the country be resolved and sovereignty and state power completely transferred to the people." It noted the "view and commitment of the CPN (Maoist) that the above mentioned goal can be achieved by holding a national political conference of the agitating democratic forces, and through its decision, forming an interim government to hold constituent assembly elections. An understanding has been reached between the agitating seven parties and the CPN (Maoist) to continue dialogue on this procedural work-list and find a common understanding." Elections announced by the king would be boycotted.

The message of the 12 Point Agreement was lost on the king. His speech on February 1, 2006, the first anniversary of his assumption of absolute control, dwelt heavily on national pride, patriotism and the shortcomings of the political parties and claimed non-existent achievements. There were also not so veiled references to external forces trying to determine Nepal's future.

Widespread public disturbances coalesced in April, 2006 in *jana andolan II* for the final denouement. The nation was brought to a standstill as people demanded the restoration of democracy. While substance and impetus was given by parties of the Seven Party alliance and the Maoists, it was also a movement of people unaffiliated with parties. Lives were lost. Perhaps the most telling definition of the movement comes from the image of a woman, wife of a soldier in the Royal Nepal Army, leading a demonstration and claiming that she was discharging her duty to her nation, as her husband was to his employer. Using the army to quell the disturbances was not an option, and nor was the army chief willing to oblige. India sent an emissary, Dr. Karan Singh, to discuss the situation with the king. On April 21, Gyanendra offered to hand over executive authority to a prime minister chosen by the Seven Party Alliance — "Executive power of the Kingdom of Nepal, which was in our safekeeping, shall, from this day, be returned to the people." Hastily welcomed by India, the offer was rejected outright by the people, giving the Seven Party Alliance no opportunity to react to it, except for a call to continue the agitation. Following strong criticism from Nepal to the Indian reaction, Indian Foreign Secretary Shyam Saran clarified in a televised press interaction on April 22 that it was entirely for the people of Nepal to decide on how they would like democracy to be restored. With regard to the traditional Indian support for the twin pillars of Nepal's polity, constitutional monarchy and multi-party democracy, the foreign secretary clarified that this had been a reflection of what the people of Nepal had desired and it was up to them entirely to decide on their future. As violent demonstrations continued, Gyanendra capitulated on April 24. Acknowledging "that the source of State Authority and Sovereignty of the Kingdom of Nepal is inherent in the people of Nepal," he recalled the parliament he had dissolved in 2002. Maoists agreed to participate in the new dispensation after a few days.

jana andolan II was the second instance in South Asia where an autocratic ruler was brought down by a genuine people's movement. The previous occasion was the street movement in Dhaka in 1990, forcing the resignation of Ershad. But whereas the anti-Ershad movement was largely centred in the capital, Nepal's movement had countrywide resonance. Also, unlike in Bangladesh, the Nepali movement presaged not only the removal of an individual, but a change in the ethos of the nation. This had implications which continue to be on the anvil today.

The ensuing period until the 2008 elections to the constituent assembly had two main areas of focus. One was the future of the monarchy and the other was introducing into democratic norms of governance a party of rigid ideologies, which, till recently, spoke the language of the gun. The former had become a foregone conclusion, but the latter was a far more serious challenge.

The monarchy had been a part of Nepal's psyche. The equation of Nepal with the dynasty may have prevented a true sense of nationhood, but not many were willing to seek its removal. Even the famous 40 points of the Maoists had only sought the removal of special privileges for the king and his family. The communists had developed a mutually beneficial and cosy relationship with Mahendra, even if transactional and divorced from any ideology. The Maoists and the palace had tried to evolve a working relationship in the 90s and Prachanda had considered an alliance with the palace against democratic forces even much later. The Nepali Congress, despite its long years of struggle for democracy, was not set against the institution of monarchy. The 12 Point Agreement of 2005 had spoken, perhaps with deliberate ambiguity, of struggle against 'absolute' and 'autocratic monarchy. It may have been an ultimatum to Gyanendra, but left the door open for the institution of monarchy itself. But *jana andolan II* saw vicious lampooning of Gyanendra, showing the people's contempt. It did not help that the Crown Prince either did not have an enviable personal record. The demythification of the monarchy that had started with the palace massacre had come full circle.

Years down the line, some regrets are expressed today even by convinced democrats that the ensuing removal of the monarchy may have been an error. This simply misses the point that though Gyanendra was in the eye of the storm, the fundamental issue was that the palace was at the centre of concentric circles of power and privilege that had lasted for over two hundred years, and the replacement merely of an individual could never address the core issues of democracy and equal opportunities. There would be no question of a 'new' Nepal emerging if there was a royal occupant of Narayanhiti. Yet, there might have been a possibility of the monarchy surviving. Wise well wishers had advised Gyandendra to call for a referendum on the issue, but he chose to abide by the advice of stalwarts of the *panchayat* era, Tulsi Giri and Kirti Nidhi Bisth, whether from hubris or apprehension, it is difficult to say.

Amid some apprehensions of military intervention in favour of the king, parliament, with G. P Koirala as the prime minister, removed in May, 2006, the king as the Commander-in-Chief of the armed forces, discarded royal insignia and declared Nepal a secular state, thus removing Gyanendra's appellation as the monarch of a Hindu kingdom. A year later, as the Maoists insisted on an end of the monarchy and the declaration of a republic, muted suggestions were floated for Gyanendra's abdication in favour of his grandson. Finally, on May 28, 2008, the newly elected Constituent Assembly voted overwhelmingly for the abolition of monarchy. On June 11, shortly after the 7th anniversary of the palace massacre, which had brought him to the throne, Gyanendra left Narayanhiti palace.

Bringing the Maoists into the mainstream was a more tortuous affair. There were suspicions among the SPA as also sections of civil society about the genuineness of commitments made by the former guerrillas in favour of multi-party democracy and a free society. Occasional intemperate statements about the introduction of a 'People's Republic' fuelled apprehensions, even as the cadres remained armed. It was, obviously, a difficult period of adjustment for the Maoist leadership, which had to convince its cadres that a revolution and People's Republic was not about to happen. Also, ideologues within the party disagreed in principle with the adjustments that required to be made. Over the years, intensive discussions were held to provide for guidelines on commitments and conduct and agreements reached. Initially, these agreements were between the SPA government and the Maoists as between two contending sides, even though they had come together to bring about the changes of April, 2006. Even after joining the interim government in April, 2007, the Maoists would continue with making demands, thus contributing to the political uncertainties.

In May, 2006, the government and the Maoists signed the 25-points Cease-fire Code of Conduct. The two sides undertook "Not to attack or destroy each other's military or security installations, not to lay down mines or ambushes, not to recruit new people in one's military and not to spy against each other." Seized properties were to be returned and those displaced allowed to return home. The former commitment was to continue to be a bone of contention. In June, the two sides agreed to "transform the ceasefire into permanent peace" and approach the United Nations for "monitoring and management of the armies and arms of both government and Maoist sides for a free and fair election to the Constituent Assembly." Significantly, it announced the decision to "form an interim government accordingly; announce the dates for elections to the constituent assembly; dissolve the House of Representatives through consensus after making alternative arrangement; dissolve the People's Governments of CPN-Maoist." The road map was becoming clearer.

Prime minister Koirala made the request for UN involvement in the peace process, specifically the monitoring of the combatants and the elections, to Secretary General Ban Ki-moon in July, eliciting a sharp letter from Prachanda, claiming parity in the treatment of the Maoist cadres and Nepal army.

The six-point Agreement of November 6 contained two clauses, which continue to loom heavily over political discussions today. There was a pledge for "progressive restructuring of the state by resolving prevailing problems related with class, ethnicity, regional and gender differences." This remains to be resolved with regard to the ongoing debate on federalism. The decision to "form a high-level commission to investigate and publicise the whereabouts of citizens stated to have been disappeared by the state and the Maoists in the past" may have been implemented formally, but neither the army nor the Maoists are willing to dig up the details, or atone for the atrocities each committed on the people during the insurgency. This was followed by the Comprehensive Peace Agreement (CPA) on November 21, 2006.

The CPA tried to weave together the various strands of discussions, agreements and concerns of all parties and mark the end of conflict. Of future significance, the problems of disadvantaged classes was to be addressed by restructuring the state "on the basis of inclusiveness, democracy and progression by ending present centralized and unitary structure of the state," thus foretelling a federal set up. The earlier commitment with regard to 'disappeared' persons was further amplified. The king was to retain no authority in the governance of the country and the future of the monarchy would be decided by the first meeting of the Constituent Assembly. Maoist cadres were to be confined to seven cantonments. The arms to be surrendered by them were to be matched by an equal number from the army and these were to be kept under UN supervision.

The CPA was the culmination of the process that had started a year earlier with the 12 point agreement. It showed the resolve of the parties concerned to proceed with governance, elections and the process of constitution making, as also deal with the potentially vexed question dealing with armed Maoist cadres. It could be argued, however, that an issue like federalism, particularly in the stated parameters of giving relief to disadvantaged groups, should have been left to the constituent assembly to deliberate and decide upon. But federalism, though differently understood, was a non-negotiable issue in *madhes,* which was to erupt in widespread violence in January, 2007. The demands from *madhes* were to be a running theme in all negotiations in the coming years.

An interim constitution was promulgated in January 2007. The elections for the constituent assembly were postponed repeatedly. What had appeared to be a clear road ahead ran into turbulence. As Lok Raj Baral explains, "After joining the interim government, the CPN (M), continued to promote a strong political message that there was no place for the monarchy in his vision of governance. The interim Prime Minister G.P. Koirala of NC held a contrasting viewpoint as he appeared to vacillate on the question of the future of the monarchy. On the one hand, Koirala presided over efforts to remove the influence of the King and the palace officials over public life and publicly accepted that the republic was the most likely outcome of impending elections and on the other hand, he refused to consider an end of the monarchy and in June 2007, publicly floated (and later denied his support) for a proposal that the King might abdicate in favour of his five year old grandson to 'save' a ceremonial role for the monarchy in

Nepal *(Baral, Ibid.)*. The danger of a coup, which may lead to return of monarchy led to an amendment of the interim constitution, which allowed for the possibility that the interim parliament might declare a republic if two-thirds majority vote in the house was achieved and on the basis of clear evidence that the king and his supporters had engaged in deliberate attempts to destabilize the peace process and the forthcoming elections *(Baral, Ibid.)*. On 10th December, 2007, the Interim parliament passed a bill that made Nepal a federal republic with the Prime Minister becoming the head of the state. On May 28, 2008, the Constituent Assembly was to abolish the monarchy by an overwhelming majority.

According to the Maoists, the monarch, who had been stripped of his de facto and ceremonial powers, could try to use his traditional support base for protecting the monarchy during the CA election. The Maoists, therefore, asked for the abolition of the monarchy by the declaration of the interim parliament along with the acceptance of full proportional electoral system as against the mixed system for holding the elections to the CA. The Maoists, thus, succeeded in declaring Nepal a republic by the interim parliament on 24th December 2007, but the task to enforce the parliamentary decision was left to the CA, which would ratify the decision in the first sitting of the new parliament. Nepal had finally become a republic.

One sensitive issue surfaced and further complicated the peace process during the period. This was the question of the integration of the Maoist cadres in the army. It was politically impossible for the Maoist leadership to accept a demonstrably raw deal for their cadres and their commitment could be seen in Prachanda's letter to the UN Secretary General in August, 2006. The Maoists felt that they had an assurance on integration from the government, which took the view that integration into the army would be difficult. The opposition to this was on the ground that rebels could not be expected to be disciplined soldiers. Tradition bound Indians made a comparison with the Indian National Army. But the comparison was invalid because the INA was a defeated entity, whereas the Maoist cadres had emerged on equal terms. There was concern that a large number of Maoist inductees could indoctrinate the disciplined soldiers of the army. This again ignored the ground reality that the soldiers and the cadres came from the same background and the former were fully aware of what was transpiring in the country. There were, in fact, numerous instances of members of the same family choosing opposite sides. The arguments against induction were fuelled by the prospect of masses of cadres entering the army. The issue became further complicated with the figures of cadres announced by UNMIN, who were monitoring the peace process. UNMIN had verified 19,000 as former cadres. Eventually, the army agreed that subject to fitness, up to 6500 could be inducted into the army. Given the option of generous financial packages and rehabilitation, only about 1600 cadres finally opted to take the requisite tests for joining the army.

For several years, the question of integration of cadres had stalled the peace process. Numbers were inflated to arouse concern and little consideration given to the fact that beyond numbers, it was a matter of principle, honour and politics for some integration to take place. I recall a civil society discussion in early summer 2008 in Delhi, when the issue was in the forefront, when it had been suggested that agreeing to accept around 6000 cadres would most likely resolve the issue. This eventually transpired after three lost years of mutual recriminations. It is difficult to gauge the truth, but it has been said that contrary to the official party line, some hard-liners in the Maoist leadership were against integration, as they hoped that the cadres could, one day, again be useful for a revived insurgency. The integration finally completed the peace process that had commenced with Comprehensive Peace Agreement in November, 2006. But a detailed analysis of this issue would show how suspicions can stall progress with an absence of reason. Regrettably, as Prof. Lok Raj Baral points out, none of the prime ministers, such as G.P. Koirala, Pushpa Kamal Dahal or Madhav Kumar Nepal showed any real interest in completing the integration process, even when they knew that both constitution making and the peace process would not be complete without the process of integration.

Elections to the constituent assembly were eventually held on April 10, 2008. The Maoists had earlier pressed for the elections to be on the basis of proportional representation. It was finally agreed to have 58 per cent of the seats under the PR system and 42 per cent under the direct elections. The Maoists won 50 per cent of the directly elected seats and 28 per cent of seats under PR, with a vote share of 30 per cent, leaving the Nepali Congress and UML far behind, each gathering about 20 per cent of the vote share. Ironically, if the elections had been held on the basis of direct elections alone, as prevalent in the rest of South Asia, the Maoists may have been able to form a government on the basis of simple majority. They had sought PR as they were unsure of their ability to win very many seats directly and wanted to be assured at least of some on the basis of their share of votes.

The Maoists were not the only ones unsure of their getting many seats. There is a story that the Nepali Congress asked one of their star campaigners, a popular artist, to try and ensure a Maoist victory in some constituencies. This may be an apocryphal tale, but reflects the perception that the mainstream parties did want the Maoists to win sufficient seats so as not to be disheartened, as they had been after the elections in the 90s and taken to the wilderness and the gun. But all the predictions of the Nepalis themselves as well as foreign analysts were proved summarily wrong and the Maoists won resoundingly. By all accounts, the elections were fair. But it is claimed that though guns may not have been visible, there was a subliminal threat perception, which worked in favour of the Maoists. Even if true, this is unlikely to have affected the results so decisively. It also needs to be underlined that there was a far larger share of women, *janjatis* and *dalits* in the Maoist lists, as also younger candidates, than among the established parties. This carries a message with regard to inclusiveness, reach and future expectations. Many of the leading personalities of the NC and the UML lost, sometimes from multiple constituencies, occasionally losing their deposit. Only Madhav Kumar Nepal resigned from his party post in acknowledgement of his defeat. It is a remarkable commentary on the state of politics in Nepal that many of those, who had been summarily rejected by the voters, continue to attempt to guide the destiny of the nation.

The Maoist victory made re-thinking necessary for the others.

These were no longer misguided people, who had to be weaned into the democratic fold. They had demonstrated their support among the electorate and had become a threatening political adversary. One must wonder if the increasingly negative attitude of the other parties and an atmosphere of some co-operation being overtaken by confrontation may not have arisen from such considerations. Civil society too seemed to lose its impartial attitude. Neither did the Maoists help build themselves a positive image. The activities of the Youth Communist League and intemperate statements by hardline ideologues were matters of obvious and genuine concern.

After the elections, Prachanda became prime minister in August, 2008. He resigned in May, 2009, following the President countermanding his decision to remove General Rookmangud Katawal as chief of the Nepal army. General Katawal was known to be a staunch royalist, but the attempted dismissal on specious grounds on the eve of his retirement was an error of judgement, as Prachanda was later to admit. This brought in India tangentially as India was clearly unhappy with direct political interference with the Nepal army, particularly at a time of systemic transition. Prachanda had earlier assured India that he would not interfere with the army. This led to an extended period of anti-India agitation prompted by the Maoist leadership.

Maoists had been catapulted into the driving seat contrary to their own expectations and without any experience of the demands or discipline of governance. The leadership had to explain to their committed cadres that even though they were now the government, the promises of the future made during the years of insurgency were not about to materialize.

Prachanda was succeeded by Madhav Kumar Nepal, Jhalanath Khanal and Baburam Bhattarai until Chief Justice Regmi took charge of administration, with the approval of all the parties, in March, 2013, with the responsibility of holding elections. The Constituent Assembly had been elected for a period of two years, extended by another two, until the Supreme Court ruled that any further extension would not be permissible. Thus, Bhattarai carried on from May 2012 to March 2013, without a parliament because the political parties could neither find a successor, nor any formula under which elections could be held. Earlier, Madhav Nepal had resigned, but had to carry on for months in a caretaker capacity since no successor could be elected, as Prachanda and Ram Chandra Poudel entered the ring seven times. Prachanda would win on points, but the rules required a knock out. Not surprisingly, the inter and intra-party differences among the parties did not permit enough attention span for the task at hand, namely, the framing of a constitution. It remains to be seen how seriously the task is addressed when a new parliament cum Constituent Assembly is elected.

The committees appointed by the dissolved assembly for framing a draft constitution have completed a major part of the task. The parliament to be elected would have to decide whether or not to accept existing recommendations and move on to the unresolved issues. Clearly, starting from scratch would be an enormously time consuming process. It would need to be borne in mind that many of the draft conclusions are the result of compromises made in discussions. Thus, if there is an effort at 'cherry picking', then the skein might unravel.

One major development in Nepal's polity since *jana andolan II* has been the rise of an increasingly self assertive *madhes,* or the terai areas lying between the hills and the Gangetic plains. The area was annexed into the kingdom by the Gorkhas in their first flush of expansion. It was ceded to the East India Company in 1816 at the Treaty of Sagauli and large portions returned after 1857 as a token of thanks following assistance rendered by the Ranas in suppressing the uprising. The dhoti wearing *madhesis,* speaking Hindi or its dialects, often with family connections across the border in Bihar or UP, have never been accepted by the hill-centric ruling elite of Kathmandu as equal citizens. The famous geologist and anthropologist Harka Gurung is said to have remarked that *madhes* had to be reconciled to its status as conquered territory. In a conversation with Gyanendra before he became king, it was clear to me that he considered the *madhesis* to be under India's influence and hence, presumably, not to be quite trusted. Given these attitudes, it is not surprising that *madhesis* were targeted as Indians during the Hrithik Roshan riots of December, 2000. The *madhesis* still recall that in the past, they were obliged to carry identity documents for visiting the capital.

With 30 per cent of the population and major contribution to the nation's revenues, *madhesis* continued to face discrimination in employment in government services, including the army, inadequate investments and persisting problems on something as fundamental as citizenship. Following *jana andolan II, madhesis*, who had earlier supported the Maoists, felt that their interests were not being addressed. There followed the violent agitation of January, 2007, which virtually cut off Nepal from the rest of South Asia. It was described as "an unprecedented event parallel to *jana andolan II*.... It was a landmark event in bringing out region based ethno-nationalism as one of the prominent issues in the national discourse on restructuring the Nepali state" *(Krishna Hachchetu, Madhesi Nationalism and Restructuring the Nepali State, 2007).* In the more direct words of a Nepali journalist some years later, "Here is what the *madhesis* told the existing Nepali state: change, or perish. In specific terms, this meant political representation, substantive inclusion, reframing symbols of nationhood, and treating citizens, who wore dhoti, did not know how to speak Nepali, and had kinship links across the border, with dignity and not scorn. If the Kathmandu establishment refused to do so, it would cost the state its legitimacy and erode political authority among one third of its people. Despite hiccups, resistance by sections in the capital, and the entrenched social prejudices, the *madhes* has won the battle politically and intellectually" (Prashant Jha).

madhes is not a uniform entity. There are differences in caste and religion, with, at times, different perceptions of self interest. *madhesi* politics has become severely fractured, some splinter groups appearing to satisfy personal agendas rather than any principles or objectives. The Nepali Congress, which earlier had a strong foothold, no longer does so. The Maoists no longer enthuse. But there are bonds of common interest, and there are no differences in the conviction that *madhes* deserves a place in the Nepali sun. This irreducible demand would have to be addressed by the future constituent assembly of Nepal.

Another issue on which a final call would have to be taken is the form of governance, a Westminster type of parliamentary democracy or a presidential system in some form. With the departure of a central figure in the monarchy, and with the likelihood of the future federal structure emerging, there is merit in considering a presidential system, which can maintain a sense of balance and stability, and perhaps a unified vision. This consideration is further underlined by the less than responsible conduct of political parties and leaders over the past years. A Nepal divided into a number of units, each possibly vying for the promotion of its ethnic agenda, while parties battle it out in parliament, as has been seen recently, cannot be a comforting thought. On the other hand, the emergence of a dictator pursuing his whims would not be acceptable. Though he has lost some sheen since he emerged from the shadows eight years ago, Prachanda is undoubtedly the most 'visible' face in Nepali politics and would likely be the most favoured candidate in a presidential election, if such a system were to be agreed upon. Unfortunately, he also arouses a sense of concern among many. His latest decision, as Chairman of the party, to do away with the various party posts decided upon by the general convention of the party only recently, may have been prompted by a desire to avoid factional disputes, but does raise questions about the degree of centralised decision making in the party. The recent debates on the future form of governance seem not to have focused as much on the merits of different systems in terms of what Nepal needs, as on the underlying apprehensions with regard to an individual. It should be possible to draw upon the experience of other nations and devise a presidential system with adequate, but not crippling, checks and balances.

The elections, due in November, 2013, would elect a new parliament also acting as a constituent assembly. Results in the 2008 elections were totally unexpected. In 2013, there are perhaps no expectations. The people have been disillusioned with the cavalier treatment of their expectations by the political parties. In fact, there was apprehension of the people taking to the streets in a violent uprising after the Constituent Assembly was dissolved without delivery. The political parties themselves would be unsure of the future, given the past experience. The parties of the centre, the NC and the UML, have been signally unable to associate themselves with the aspirations for change among the people. Seen to be primarily concerned with the ambitions of the long-term leaders, they have not been able to provide the kind of leadership, which the fraught time of transition requires. As a senior NC leader told me, they are seen as the reluctant rear coach of a train moving ahead, rather than try to be the driving force. Another mentioned that no statement of a vision of Nepal's future has emanated from these parties since *jana andolan II.* There is dismay among the middle ranks of these parties at the absence of cohesive and purposeful leadership. The various agreements signed since the 12 point agreement of 2006 contain the substance of the future roadmap for Nepal. But the issues seem not to have been internalized. This is where the Maoists have an advantage, despite their internal differences, even if some would question the honesty of their commitment to democracy.

4
The Federalism Debate

The issue of federalism has dominated discussions in parliament, politics and civil society. It is likely to be the main issue of contention in the assembly to be elected. Passions have been high and that may have precluded a sober discourse.

There are half truths surrounding the debate and half truths, because they seem to appear plausible, can divert attention from basics. The Maoists are charged with promoting ethnic consciousness and assuring federalism based on ethnicity. The approach seems to be that all of Nepal was one happy family until Maoists introduced subversive ideas. Facts of history state otherwise. Various marginalized groups have been agitating for recognition and acceptance of their legitimate demands for a very long time. This had met with little or no success as the mainstream political parties, when in power, took no pains to address their grievances. The Maoists supported these aspirations and garnered support. Whether they were genuine in their stated support and convictions, or used the window of opportunity to portray themselves as agents of change, as their detractors would aver, is another matter altogether. Any possible absence of Maoist sincerity does not detract from the obvious strength and validity of the demands for inclusion and acknowledgment. Similarly, foreign anthropologists alien to local traditions are thought to have focused excessively on cultural anthropology, not always with the strictest objectivity, and even with ulterior motives, to find differences where none may have existed. Even if this may be argued, the fact also remains that questions of exclusion and the imposition of brahmanical values have been spoken of by such eminent Nepali anthropologists and thinkers as Harka Gurung and Dor Bahadur Bista. And anthropological research besides, facts speak for themselves. Marginalised social groups have only marginal share, let alone proportionate, in the legislature, executive, judiciary, media or even civil society. Their exclusion from the national mainstream is no abstract theory or political gamesmanship, but visible in all studies, including the Planning Commission's documents, and is a fact recognised by the interim constitution.

Though constrained by the laws banning political activity under the *panchayat* regime, a number of ethnic organizations had sprung up over time concentrating on social and cultural matters. A combination of ethnic organizations formed the MAGURALI, later enlarging to SHETA MAGURALI, in the early 80s, believed to have been encouraged by the palace to support the *panchayati raj,* though Prof. Baral believes that they wanted to 'remind' Birendra that they formed the core of the army from the time of his ancestors and could change the balance of power. The Mongol National Organisation founded in 1989 had demanded a secular, federal state. It is noteworthy that when the 1990 constitution came into being, most ethnic groups abstained from the celebrations, as it did not represent a change for them. These and other autonomous developments were brewing well before their cause was embraced by the Maoists. Senior politicians have told me that the democratic governments after 1990 were impervious to the gathering demands from the ethnic minorities, G.P. Koirala being among the most indifferent.

It is, obviously, a complex subject, but the core issues must be kept in mind. A factor, which complicates the debate further is that the demand for 'federalism' is not based on the same premises by different groups among, for example, the *janjatis* and the *madhesis*. The former want to affirm their distinct identity and to be treated as equals. The latter want to ensure that the humiliations of past rule from Kathmandu, which virtually identified the state with the hills, are never repeated and wish to manage their affairs in a federation within Nepal. Neither have any wish to separate from the state of Nepal. In this context, Kanak Mani Dixit makes a significant point, "People of Terai origin, who constitute a large proportion of the total population, have finally begun to feel a sense of ownership of the nation-state of Nepal" *(Kanak Mani Dixit, Peace Politics of Nepal, Himal Books, 2011)*. Thus interpreted, *madhesi* self assertion strengthens any new sense of Nepali nationhood.

With regard to *janjatis*, the origins of the problem lie in the Muluki Ain introduced by Jang Bahadur Rana in 1864. The intention may have been to bring together the disparate regions and their peoples, recently conquered and integrated into the kingdom of Nepal, under a common code, which drew from ancient Hindu texts, some local practices and even from prevalent laws in India. In effect, however, a large number of groups were brought into the Hindu fold by fiat with a subordinate, if not subservient, status, and has been seen by ethnic groups as the principal cause for future disparities. Caste was introduced among peoples whose traditions had no caste. Seen in the context of the times, the intentions may not have been malicious or Machiavellian, but continued to rankle as a focal point of disaffection. It certainly tried to perpetuate the privileged position of the ruling classes. As Dixit puts it, "The Muluki Ain may have been devised as a means to bring order amidst the diversity of caste-ethnic interface that was Nepali society, but it locked communities into straitjackets of disenfranchisement for more than a century" *(Kanak Mani Dixit, Peace Politics of Nepal, Himal Books, 2011)*.

According to Prof. Lok Raj Baral, "The psychology of the Nepali rulers had always been guided by the idea that the assimilation of all minorities and social groups into the broad Gorkhali culture would be the rock bottom of the modern Nepali state...... Assimilation fitted into the Gorkhali agenda of domination by one group of people over the other...." *(Lok Raj Baral, Nepal, Nation State in the Wilderness, Sage, 2012)*.

The Muluki Ain formalized a codified stratification where, in large parts of a multi-faceted country, such distinctions were unknown. This was to eventually transform to reaction, as succinctly put by Dor Bahadur Bista. "The upper caste-class people must realize that they are merely one of the elements within this pluralism. They too are an ethnic minority. They should not insist on the imposition of the values of one minority over the others as a solution, especially where the values are manifested in a social hierarchy with themselves at the top and the others at the bottom....... The others have resisted this solution for two thousand years. This is the only way they could maintain their dignity and self respect. Nepali people's self respect and dignity cannot be maintained when the small number of upper caste-class people consistently treat the majority as lower in the hierarchical order. The only product of this was resentment, a retreat away from national into ethnic identity, and a sense of resentment, even hostility, to the state...... Minority people struggle for an identity, and demand that the identity be publicly acknowledged as having import" *(Dor Bahadur Bista, Fatalism and Development, Orient Longmans, 2008).*

Even though the Muluki Ain was modified in 1964, the after effects and the bitter taste remain and are now manifested in the federalism debate.

But if there was some glimmer of understanding of the angst among the *janjatis,* the discrimination against *madhes* went largely unnoticed to outsiders. Here (refer chapter three), there was systematic and systemic denial of equal rights to a significant part of the population. *madhes* erupted in January, 2007. The earlier conciliatory and reasoned approach of the Sadbhavna Party was now overtaken by newer parties with far greater assertiveness with no hesitation in adopting violent means to achieve their objectives. Federalism, signifying the right of the people to guide their own affairs was now a sine qua non. It is the *madhesi* demand for federalism that has ensured that there would be no backtracking on the principle. On this issue, the *janjatis* and the *madhesis* have made common cause, even if the essence of their demands may vary, and the former have not hesitated to sever their links with mainstream parties if their demands were not met, as happened with the UML. It has been noticed that the major hill based parties lost their ardour for federalism, once the federalism debate centred on *madhes*. But, by then, the *janjatis* in their own backyard had become intractable.

The debate on federalism has become heavily politicized with 'fundamentalists' on both sides of the divide. Those who would like the continuation of an unitary state emphasise the pitfalls of 'ethnic' federalism, the fact that there are no areas where any group would be in a majority or that in any such unit, the minorities would be disadvantaged leading to future strifes. Those claiming rights and privileged positions in defined areas for individual groups are unable to square the circle of their own contradictions. The committees appointed by the Constituent Assembly had made a number of suggestions, which could be the starting point for future deliberations. A middle ground had appeared to tentatively emerge in May, 2011, but was stilled by the dissolution of the last Constituent Assembly.

With the emergence of extreme positions, the issue has been polarised. What has to be accepted is that with the developments over the past years, a discussion on whether or not federalism is good for Nepal is infructuous. However well intentioned, any attempt to reopen this question would only deepen suspicions. What is essential is to determine a future federal structure of Nepal that would reflect at least the minimum acceptable demands of the people without damaging either the edifice of the state or social harmony. The economic viability of the federating units is a factor to be taken into account.

While it is the internal dynamics of the Nepali polity that would determine the outcome, two external views may be noted. India is supportive of the *madhesi* demand for federalism in whatever form may be decided. In a departure from their usual practice of not commenting on the internal developments in Nepal, China has publicly spoken against federalism in Nepal. They would prefer to deal with a central authority, particularly with regard to their Tibetan concerns. With multiple states which, China fears, could be individually wooed by western powers, China's ability to influence policies in Nepal via a central Kathmandu based controlling authority, may be diminished.

It is likely that the federalism debate would figure prominently in the forthcoming elections in November, 2013. For the future of Nepal, the issue should be addressed with maturity by all concerned. It is an issue on which passions have been, and can continue to be, aroused. There is, undoubtedly, merit in the argument that federalism is not a panacea for ending deprivation or ensuring progress, and what is required is affirmative action. But people whose legitimate demands have been long denied and ignored are no longer willing to accept assurances at face value. They have to be made to feel that in some significant way, they can mould their own futures and be allowed full participation in governance of the nation. As a broad-brush comparison with a neighbour, we may observe that despite the benefit of democratic governance and numerous affirmative actions over the decades, of which the Mandal Commission acquired the highest profile, despite the safeguards afforded to the small states in the north-east, India is still some way from achieving a society where all feel equal. The shadows of the past cannot be wiped away by legislation alone and time has to provide the final closure. For Nepal, thrust into a virtual maelstrom of demands erupting after centuries of a rigid and codified feudal order, the challenges are truly massive. How to strike a desirable balance between politics, economics and administration and channel passions constructively is the challenge today before the political parties and groups in Nepal.

5
The Hrithik Roshan Affair

Reports of sporadic protests about the alleged anti-Nepal statement of actor Hrithik Roshan had been coming in, but there was no indication of the proportions it might assume and the explosion one would witness in the capital. I had planned a week's trek to the area north of the Valley in the company of friends visiting from India. We left early on the morning of December 26 for Sundarijal where the trail started and reached Chisopani at the crest of the hills to the north of Kathmandu in the afternoon. Very early the following morning, as I was getting ready for the days trek, there was a knock on my door at the guest house. An inspector of police saluted and informed me that there had been disturbances in the valley the previous day (those were days before mobiles and I was not yet equipped with a satellite phone) and the Inspector General of police wanted me to return to the capital immediately. The shortest way would have been the way we had come. But this was no longer safe as the area below was particularly disturbed. I was advised that we should walk east to Nagarkot, the well known hill station, about twenty kilometres away along the same ridge as Chisopani, and enter Kathmandu when circumstances permitted via Bhaktapur. We reached Nagarkot under armed escort about four in the afternoon, but were advised to wait till the situation in the valley was considered safe. The Superintendent of Police from Bhaktapur escorted us down late in the evening and we reached Kathmandu about 10 in the evening, passing areas marked by vandalism and still smouldering tyres on the road.

The Indian media (later to describe me as the absent envoy)

arrived in a day or so and wanted the ambassador to address the people of Nepal on television to restore calm. I thought that this could well have the opposite effect and it would be best left to the government to deal with the situation. Prime Minister Vajpayee called me to express his concern and enquire about the ground situation. He also called Prime Minister Koirala and when I met him later in the day, he appeared unhappy that I had told my prime minister that PM Koirala had been ineffective in dealing with the situation. This was far from the truth, for the government had been doing its best since the violence erupted, but had, by now, itself become a target of political parties and individuals within the ruling party. Somehow, I do not think G.P. Koirala ever forgave me for having 'complained' to my prime minister. The fact remains that neither the Nepali, nor the Indian establishments, or their agencies, had any clue about what was afoot before the disturbances erupted on December 26. It had been a success for the organizers of the troubles.

Violent exhibition of anti-Indian feelings have been seen occasionally in Nepal over the past many decades. From the late 50s, issues or non-issues with regard to India would be fomented by political formations to stress Nepal's nationhood and sovereignty. These were largely confined to the Valley. The last such demonstration of 'people's anger' was organized by the Maoists in 2009.

The Hrithik Roshan riots of December 2000 were the most widespread of anti-Indian demonstrations. Though lasting only two days in its intensity, it left scars and questions answered and not answered. The riots targeted Indian institutions and *madhesis* in the unspoken but unmistakable message that they were considered no different from Indians. At a multi-party public meeting to establish harmony a few days later, a leading member of the Rashtriya Prajatantra Party (the Palace party) had described the disturbances as an '*andolan*' (movement), to which Gajendra Narain Singh of the Sadbhavna Party had retorted that it would be more appropriate to describe it as '*atyachar*' (brutal oppression).

The riots gave a jolt to Indo-Nepal relations, coming as it did on the anniversary of the hijacking of Indian Airlines flight IC 814 in Kathmandu by terrorists with Pakistan links. Most political parties fell in line in trying to take advantage of the situation for their immediate perceived gains. It needs to be noted that the agitation and subsequent violence took place while 'Mission Kashmir', a film on the theme of Pakistan inspired terrorism in Kashmir, starring Hrithik Roshan, was drawing large audiences and among the first targets was the cinema hall showing the film in Kathmandu. Collusion between activists controlled by the palace, happy to discredit the government and cause rifts with India, and ISI operatives has been widely surmised. Given the dubious distinction of those few days in the history of Indo-Nepal relations, a recapitulation of the events as reported is useful both as a record of the times with also lessons to be drawn. The following extracts from some of the comments and reportage of the events provide both an account as also the flavour of the days:

> "If we needed a proof of just how volatile Nepal's political scene has become, then this week was it. A rumour that Indian actor Hrithik Roshan had slandered Nepal in a television show on 14 December spread like wildfire, triggering riots and demonstrations all over the country. No matter that Roshan himself denied ever having insulted Nepalis. But the damage had been done. Street unrest took on a momentum of its own. Congress factions emboldened by the crisis smelt blood. A group of five Leftist student unions saw this as an opportunity to boost their agitation. Little-known Rightists spread leaflets demanding the restoration of "nationalist" rulers. In the wings, the Maoists benefited from the escalating atmosphere of anarchy."
>
> (*Nepali Times*, 28 December 2001-3 January 2002)

"The first news about the protests by some youths in Chitwan against Indian actor Hrithik Roshan was carried out by a small town Nepali language Newspaper called the '*Chitwan Post*' on 15th December 2000. The newspaper reported that a section of Chitwan youth had burnt the effigy of the actor, believing that he had expressed dislike towards 'Nepal and Nepalis' (*www.himal.mag*).

This news was later picked by the mainstream media without verification.

The attitude of the demonstrators has been pithily summarized by Pratyoush Onta:

"They said, 'Hrithik Roshan insulted Nepal. We should avenge that insult. Burn his posters on the streets, tear up his postcards. Torch his film and the movie hall where it is being screened.'

"You ask for proof that Hrithik actually said it? The people on the streets do not need proof!"

"Hrithik is India. India is our big brother. Big brother imperialist! Respect our sovereignty! Go home big brother India!

"Burn tyres! Show your love for the Nepali nation!"

"Anti-India means anybody looking Indian must not be spared. Is this the house of Mr so-and-so?" (*Pratyoush Onta, "The Paradox of the Nepali Mindset: Hate India, Love India," February 2001, Himal - South Asian*).

The Kathmandu Post, one of the most widely circulated newspapers in Nepal, wrote, "The spontaneous outburst of the students and the youth community against alleged anti-Nepal remarks by an Indian actor goes to show how deeply Nepalis feel about their country and the people." In a later editorial, the *Kathmandu Post* tried to put up a defence saying that what it had done was "to report the events that took place."

"Without introspection as to how the national press as a whole (and mostly, of course, the vernacular media) had triggered the events in the first place. It was on this high and self-righteous moral ground of objective reporting that responsible journalism met its nemesis in the newsrooms and editorial desks of Kathmandu (*www.himal.mag*).

"In Kathmandu, the protests heated up from 26th December 2000. The mob took the protests in front of the Indian Embassy when riots broke out, which spread all over the city. The police force claimed that they couldn't control the angry mob with tear gas and lathi charges, therefore, resorting to the use of live bullets, in order to bring some sort of discipline in the streets. This led to the death of more than 4 people, which included a 12 year old girl, who was hit by a stray bullet. Violence also broke out in the major part of the city such as New Road, Thamel, Chabahil and New Baneshwor among other places, where vehicles were set on fire and shops vandalized. Movies starring the actor had been banned and the cable TV networks had also at the time stopped broadcasting Indian channels (*www. Wavemag.com*).

While numerous international media agencies reported that all of Kathmandu Valley was ruled by violent mobs during those two days, in reality, only certain areas in Kathmandu were seriously affected. There were, however, disturbances elsewhere as well, including the terai, and *madhesis* were targeted.

What had started as demonstrations against an actor, soon turned into agitation against Indians (and violence against Indian interests). It then expanded to include attacks on the government in which fringe communists, Maoists and hard-core royalists participated. Strangely, even senior members of established political parties took the opportunity to attack the Koirala government on the issue. It helped those, who were out to discredit a democratic government.

"While Hrithik Roshan vehemently denied reports that quoted him making insensitive remarks about Nepalese, the Channel Star Plus, which aired the interview, seconded the actor's story. Terming the accusations as baseless and 'ludicrous', Hrithik refused to cede to the demands of those asking an apology from him. He instead declared that he had 'absolute regard for Nepal' and would never venture into hurting sentiments of the people of the Nepali community" (*Rajeev Masand, Indian Express, 2000*).

"Defending his side, Hrithik called the incident to be deliberately designed by figment of imagination of some vested interests to tarnish his image, and also gave matter of doubt that competitors were trying to ruin his reputation" (*Asia News Agency, ABC News*).

Other speculations included the hand of Dawood Ibrahim getting his own back on the Indian actor as part of a longstanding feud with the Roshan family. While Dawood may have encouraged his henchmen, this answer is too simplistic.

Many years later, I revisited the events with an official, who had been in the heart of the establishment at the time. He reconfirmed that the riots had been engineered by the palace and Pakistan to discredit the government and cause rifts with India.

The Hrithik Roshan riots have been interpreted by some to indicate that the extreme levels of anti-Indianism latent in the Nepali psyche may find such outlets at any time, given a suitable opportunity. Certain levels of concern about India, or anti-Indianism, may be present, but it is neither ingrained nor explosive. While that is a separate matter for consideration, what the Hrithik Roshan riots did demonstrate is that given ruthless determination, serious trouble can be engineered by a relatively small number of people acting under the orders of a calculating authority. The reaction of elements of the political classes showed an unfortunate inclination to garner political benefits from a difficult situation, as evidenced by the attack on the government by members of the ruling party itself. The comment of the chairperson of the Parliamentary Foreign Relations Committee in Nepal, Som Prasad Pandey of the UML, that the main reason for the outbreak of violence was the encroachment on Nepali land and the dams India has set up without Nepal's consent on border rivers, is also indicative of the ultra nationalism that was brought into play by those from whom a greater sense of responsibility could have been expected.

Tanka Bahadur Subba, the noted anthropologist said in the aftermath of the violence, "In order to illustrate how the lives of the two communities are intertwined, it is worth noting that Nepali-speakers of India are increasingly held answerable for what Nepal is perceived to be doing, and what 'happens' to Indians in Nepal. A glaring instance was the attack on some Indians and 'Indian-looking' people on the streets of Kathmandu in December 2000 in the wake of the unsubstantiated rumour that a Hindi film actor had made some anti-Nepal comments. While there was no backlash against Nepali-speakers across the length of India that some felt could have occurred, it came too close for comfort. Hopefully the so-called 'Hrithik Roshan incident' will lead to some sensitivity among Nepal's politicians in future before they go about inflaming passions against 'Indians' on Kathmandu streets. The state of bilateral relations between the two countries on either side of the border, and for this reason alone, the Kathmandu intelligentsia must realize that Nepal cannot absolve itself of its responsibility towards the large Nepali-speaking population in India, be they Indian citizens. And, like it or not, even they try to create an Indian reality for themselves, the latter too must understand that they are bound to be affected by actions taken by and within Nepal (*Tanka Bahadur Subba, Nepal and the Indian Nepalis from State of Nepal, edited by Kanak Mani Dixit and Shastri Ramachandran, Himal Books, 2002*).

Subba's concern about a backlash in India against Nepali nationals or Nepali speaking Indians if such incidents recur and his caution to Nepali political classes in showing restraint while inflaming anti-Indian passions is timely. While they may not feel responsible for Nepali speaking Indians, they must appreciate the possible consequences for millions of Nepali nationals, who earn a living in India. In the tense days following the riots, this concern had also been expressed to me by some responsible Nepali politicians. The Maoists were treading on thin ice when they organized anti-Indian demonstrations in 2009 and 2010. These were intended to target the state, but the dividing line when this targets nationals and establishments can become blurred.

In Shastri Ramachandran's analysis, "As nationalist feeling ran high, political elements raised the frenzy to a new level. The end result was once again to prove to the Indian public that the depths of anti-India feeling runs high in the minds of the psyche and which can anytime explode" (*Shastri Ramachandran, "Nepal as Seen from India," India International Quarterly, 2003*).

This could be correct in terms of cause and effect, but the fact is that the Hrithik Roshan riots were not a spontaneous outburst of Nepali nationalism, but organized and orchestrated with malafide intent by forces inimical both to the democratically elected government of Nepal and Indo-Nepal relations with lumpen elements as their storm troopers. Regrettable as the riots were, also most unfortunate was the ultra nationalist stand taken by sections of the political classes and the media with little regard to facts or concern for possible consequences.

6
India and Nepal

The relations between India and Nepal are generally described as unique. The open border, national treatment granted to the nationals of each other (even though there is imbalance in how each country implements the facility) and the long existing familial links at various levels, do underline the extraordinary relations between the two sovereign states, even if these may not always have translated into closeness in political relations. India has a direct interest in the development of water resources in Nepal. Besides industrial ventures, this is one area where Indian involvement in terms of collaboration with Nepal is possible. There are areas where developments in Nepal could impinge negatively on India's security. These may be described as areas of concern, which are no less matters of vital Indian national interest, even if India's ability to influence outcomes may be limited. It is believed in Nepal that relations with India are a major factor in its internal politics. It is also a converse reality that Indo-Nepal relations have been, and will continue to be, influenced by the shape of internal political developments in Nepal. There is a running thread of permanence in India's interests and concerns vis-à-vis Nepal and what is valid today will be so in the foreseeable future.

Indo-Nepal relations are at multiple layers. The traditional elite of Nepal, the Ranas and the Shahs, who trace their origins to India going back a few hundred years, continue to have matrimonial linkages with erstwhile princely families of India. The *madhesis* have similar linkages with Bihar and UP, *roti beti ka rishta*, as they say. Millions of hill Nepalis work in India and many have family links with Indian citizens of Nepali origin. During the insurgency, many

Nepali citizens fled to India from remote villages to avoid being caught by the twin dangers of Maobadi demands and army action. The chief of the Nepal Army is an honourary general of the Indian army, an honour reciprocated by Nepal. Nepali Gorkhas fight in the Indian army for the cause of India. Each of the elements of this relationship is important, but none represents the whole by itself. To describe the relationship of Nepal and India as unique is an understatement. What this also emphatically underlines is that while relations between states occupies much of our attention and analysis, in the case of Indo-Nepal relations, the many connectivities among people can and do play a significant role.

All neighbours are important in their own way for all countries. Nepal's location adjoining the flat Gangetic plains of India, with China to the north, has clear security implications. India must also recognize that Nepal's geographical location poses for itself even greater security concerns. It is all very well for the Nepali to play the China card that preys on the Indian mind. It is quite another to move into any close embrace of Beijing, having had a ringside view of the fate of Tibet. Nor is it necessary for Nepal to consider any such choice. As far as India is concerned, while its size may be daunting, the Indian psyche has neither the attitude nor the ruthlessness to pursue a policy of domination. Sikkim may be geographically close to Nepal, but its absorption into India, which is referred to as indicative of the dangers that confront Nepal, had very different historical and geo-political backgrounds. Neither did India display any acquisitive approach to Nepal when it may have been possible to do so in the unsettled years after 1947. The best guarantee of India's interests in Nepal is the flourishing of independent Nepali nationalism that is able to look at choices and pursue a course beneficial for the people. And it is the people who should be the determining factor, for their genuine welfare cannot be divorced from a co-operative relationship with India.

Security has other elements as well. A disturbed state in Nepal would mean an even larger influx of temporary or permanent refugees into India. There are large numbers of Nepali speaking Indian citizens in Sikkim, West Bengal and in the north-east. Events in Nepal will impact on them. In the past, it was from Indian soil that agitations were carried out against the established order in Nepal, and the nature of the border and the existing connectivities have, and will, make this inevitable if there is repression. The Maobadi insurgency was the first that was entirely home-grown and without external support or inspiration. Instability or uncertainty in Nepal has, therefore, very direct consequences for India.

From India's point of view, it needs to be recognized that new elements have emerged in Nepal in the past few decades. The movement of people and the reach of the media, particularly the radio, have made people more conscious of the world outside and more conscious of their rights. The consequences of the Maoist insurgency went beyond mere ideology or the means to power. It focused on the essential needs and concerns of many and conveyed to people in distant corners that there is a commonality in their problems and aspirations. Nepal has irrevocably graduated from being identified with a Hindu monarchy and is attempting to forge itself into a nation state.

A parallel development has been the emergence of an assertive middle class, unknown half a century ago, with no particular emotional association with or attachment to India, and able to look at issues from a nationalist Nepali point of view. This self-assurance is reflected in the remarkably courageous press. They are suspicious of politicians who, despite their creditable fight for democracy before 1990, and again recently, have been immersed in the politics of manoeuvres. They are resentful of what they perceive as India's patronizing attitudes. As a former Nepali research scholar in a leading Indian university wrote, the Indians "think that we Nepalis are not capable of becoming more than private guards, mercenaries, and servants working in dhabas, hotels and restaurants. And they think the king is the lord of a man-power company called Nepal." An eminent author has commented that India is unable to distinguish between the sovereign state of Nepal and its own neglected states in the north-east. This sense of hurt to a new pride in the nation has to be recognized and assuaged.

The question of anti-Indian feelings in Nepal has been of concern to India (see Chapter Five). A conscious policy of equating Nepali nationalism with anti-Indianism was evolved by the palace after Mahendra's coup of 1960. The king, by virtue of the conquest of the territory by his ancestors, was the sole guarantor of Nepali independence, to which India was a threat. QED. A line of reasoning not dissimilar to what is propagated by the Pakistan army to retain its privileged position. Several statements of King Gyanendra touched on the same theme. In sum, power to the palace was necessary to save Nepal from the ugly Indian. In a sense, of course, the argument had merit. The British had come to a mutually advantageous arrangement with the Nepali elite and were not concerned with the Nepali people (The Chinese have a similar approach, substituting elite with ruling establishment). A democratic India could not be indifferent to the people and, to that extent, did pose a threat to established privileges by simply being there, besides the moral support which India did, indeed, extend to democratic forces.

An additional point was brought into focus by scholars in the 60s. "Independent India was a far greater challenge to Nepal's national integrity then the British rulers of India. The latter had posed a political problem, which had been threatening only on rare occasions... Indian influence at all levels — political, economic, cultural and religious — is so pervasive that the Nepalis have to struggle continually against absorption into the 'mother culture'. Nepalis were bound to be strongly agitated by the Indian threat to their political integrity, no matter how 'benevolent' and 'altruistic' the Indian authorities may have been in their attitude to Nepal" (Prof. Leo Rose). This is a valid point, but, in retrospect, a valley-centric assessment, as the many agitating ethnic groups today have no apprehensions of being absorbed by any Indian 'mother culture'.

Besides committed royalists, Mahendra reached out to the communists. The primary intent would have been to neutralize centrist democratic forces, then represented by the Nepali Congress, but the promotion of anti-Indian sentiments was also part of the agenda and, in course of time, this became ingrained in communist folklore. Even till the late 90s, the UML was to agitate against 'Indian expansionism', which still perhaps remains a bogey to be utilized as required.

A frequently discussed element of Indo-Nepal relations is the 1950 Treaty of Peace and Friendship. Over time, the treaty has been the subject of severe criticism in Nepal. There have been calls for its abrogation or change by all political parties, some, as with the Maoists, with greater stridency. It had featured in the 40-point list of demands by the Communist Party of Nepal (Maoist) in 1996, as well as in the party's manifesto prior to the 2008 elections. The emphasis had been on removing 'unequal' elements, and not on 'scrapping' the agreement outright — a term that is occasionally in evidence, though it is difficult to segregate official policy statements from casual reporting by the media.

It needs to be recalled that, though the CPN (Maoist) has consistently emphasised the importance it attaches to changes in (or elimination of) treaties or agreements with India that they consider to be unequal; such views have been expressed by all major political parties in Nepal over the years. For its part, India's stance has been that it is prepared to discuss all options — namely, continuation, termination (as is provided for in the agreement itself), or the negotiation of a new treaty. Indeed, some drafts for a revised treaty were prepared by both sides a decade or more ago, but there has been no meaningful discussion to take the matter forward

There could well be differences of perception regarding the origins of the treaty. But judged from a distance, such perceptions may not always take into account the international, regional, national and bilateral circumstances in which the treaty was formulated and signed. Or, indeed, it's possible importance today.

At the time, it may have been useful for Nepal to have a successor treaty to the Anglo-Nepal Treaty of 1923, which, as Nepal had conveyed to the United Nations in 1949, had confirmed Nepal's sovereignty and independence. Seen from this perspective, the 1950 treaty, which (Article 8) overtook all Anglo-Nepal treaties, was an affirmation of Nepal's sovereignty by India.

India's concern vis-à-vis the possible regional fallout of the developments in China in the context of the time is well documented. Writing to the Prime Minister of Burma in January 1950, Jawaharlal Nehru had said, "There is not much danger of any Chinese aggression across the Indian border. But I want to make it quite clear, if occasion arises, that the slightest attempt at such aggression whether in Nepal or India would be stoutly resisted by us." Nehru had advised against the formation of anti-Chinese blocs, which could aggravate the situation. There was a similar refrain in Nehru's letter to Indian chief ministers, and his statement in the Indian parliament in March 1950.

The first Chinese occupation of Tibet was then only months away, and Kathmandu was explaining to the UN a year earlier that the 1792 Sino-Nepal Treaty (which had described Nepal and Tibet as two brothers, to whom China was the father) was now obsolete. In such an environment, it is possible that Nepal too may have felt some disquiet over regional developments and a need for affirmation and acknowledgement of its sovereign status.

The treaty was concluded with a discredited Rana regime, then under considerable nationalist pressure and living out its last days — a memory that has since sustained Nepali suspicions. Also, the fact that the Indian ambassador at the time was a signatory may be post facto hurtful to Nepali national pride. But it can also be seen in the context of the 1923 Anglo-Nepal Treaty, which was signed by a British lieutenant-colonel, who had been elevated from being the British resident to envoy.

All of this is of little relevance in today's context. Three essentials do, however, need to be underlined. First, a treaty is relevant and valid as long as both parties are comfortable with it, and as long as both are in agreement to honour at least its broad parameters. Second, to a greater or lesser extent, neither India nor Nepal has abided by the letter of the treaty. Third, internal — particularly in Nepal — as well as regional and international conditions have changed so greatly over the past six decades that a fresh look at the treaty is not only inevitable, but also desirable. An informed understanding of the treaty is important so that an entirely needless irritant is cauterised.

History is replete with instances of treaties remaining valid only so long as the parties find it useful. Their importance often lies in the moment of their signing, underlining immediate mutual concerns. When these concerns fade away, so does the relevance of the treaty. The 1971 Indo-Soviet Treaty has to be seen in the context of the crisis in East Pakistan and the looming war clouds with unqualified Chinese and US support for Pakistan. The Indo-Bangladesh Treaty of 1972 reflected the relations at the time and reaffirmed Indian commitment to the sovereignty of Bangladesh even as she, at the time, remained unaccepted by large and influential sections of the international community. It is instructive to recall that with political changes in Bangladesh after 1975, this treaty too was depicted as an Indian design on the sovereignty of Bangladesh and continued to be a favourite political slogan until it expired unsung and unmourned in the fullness of time in 1997. Unlike such treaties, however, the 1950 treaty envisages permanent connectivities and some of its clauses have serious legal connotations on issues like national treatment. It is not a document to be brushed aside by political whims.

The 1950 Treaty contains no clauses that are detrimental to Nepal's sovereignty. The aspects of security and consultations mentioned in the treaty were perhaps more necessary for Nepal then with the Chinese occupation of Tibet, and were, in fact, less detailed than the terms of Nepal's 1923 Treaty with Britain. The somewhat convoluted article III of the 1923 treaty reads, "As the preservation of peace and friendly relations with the neighbouring States whose territories adjoin their common frontiers is to the mutual interests of both the High Contracting Parties, they hereby agree to inform each other of any rupture in such friendly relations, and each to exert its good offices as far as may be possible to remove such friction and misunderstanding". Article 2 of the 1950 treaty is more direct, "The two Governments hereby undertake to inform each other of any serious friction or misunderstanding with any neighbouring State likely to cause any breach in the friendly relations subsisting between the two Governments." Concern about neighbouring state is evident in both and the 1950 side letter is quite explicit, "Neither Government shall tolerate any threat to the security of the other by a foreign aggressor. To deal with any such threat, the two Governments shall consult with each other and devise effective countermeasures."

As Nepal grew in self assurance, these clauses came to be depicted as, in some way, restricting Nepal's freedom of action. It is a fact that till the mid-fifties, Nepal thought fit to be guided by India on foreign policy. But, unlike in the case of Bhutan, this was not obligatory in any treaty terms. In reality, Nepal has very much followed an independent foreign policy including playing the China card after 1962 and being in sympathy for Pakistan in 1971. At the time, however, Nepal and India had close military co-operation and India was permitted a presence at Nepal's northern borders with Tibet, an arrangement which ceased in the 60s.

An important addition to the 1923 treaty was article 6, which stated, "Each Government undertakes, in token of the neighbourly friendship between India and Nepal, to give to the nationals of the other, in its territory, national treatment with regard to participation in industrial and economic development of such territory and to the grant of concessions and contracts relating to such development." This was modified in the side letter which stated, "The Government of India recognize that it may be necessary for some time to come to afford the Nepalese nationals in Nepal protection from unrestricted competition. The nature and extent of this protection will be determined as and when required by mutual agreement between the two Governments." One observes that despite such a clause, there was widespread objection in Nepal to the conclusion even of the Bilateral Investment Protection Agreement proposed by the Bhattarai government in 2011.

The crucial addition to the 1923 treaty is article 7, which states, "The Governments of India and Nepal agree to grant, on a reciprocal basis, to the nationals of one country in the territories of the other the same privileges in the matter of residence, ownership of property, participation in trade and commerce, movement and other privileges of a similar nature." This has remained largely a one way facility.

As such, then, as far as benefits and observance are concerned, the treaty would appear to be dispensable from the Indian point of view. Whether this is politically desirable is another matter.

In November, 2000, I had said at the Nepal Council for World Affairs in response to criticism of the Treaty, that clause 10 of the

Treaty permitted either country to terminate it with an year's notice and Nepal could certainly do so if it found the terms of the Treaty to be onerous or unacceptable. My comment had been considered 'harsh' by some. Responding to Nepali suggestions for changes in the Treaty at the Foreign Office talks in January, 2001, India had said that it was willing to consider all options, namely continuation, termination or re-negotiation.

The 1950 Treaty of Peace and Friendship between India and Nepal is unlike a host of such treaties, which dot the diplomatic landscape. Most are significant in terms of the circumstances surrounding their timing, e.g., the Indo Soviet Treaty of 1971 or the Indo-Bangladesh Treaty of 1972. They express the mutual intent and inter-dependence of the parties at a given point of time, may serve as a warning to others, but, unlike the 1950 treaty, impose no specific permanent obligations on the parties.

The problem in dispensing with the treaty would arise in particular with regard to the millions of Nepali nationals in India being accorded very largely national treatment. Abrogation of the treaty would thus place the Nepali nationals in India, enjoying in many respects the rights of an Indian citizen, in an impossible legal situation. There are suggestions, including from well-meaning Indians, that Nepali nationals could be accorded existing facilities even without a treaty. Without a covering framework, this will not be legally sustainable. Even as the present treaty may confer little benefit to India, she would not, politically, be able to enter into a new treaty with explicit advantages to Nepal alone. Nor would this be acceptable to Nepali nationalists. The issue has been skirted by letting the treaty quietly hibernate, and this may well remain the best course. However, should any future Nepali dispensation seek to raise the issue with any seriousness, all implications of termination as also the obligations of each state in any new treaty, would need to be most carefully gone through. The only "unequal stipulation or agreement" in the Treaty is, in fact, in favour of Nepal with regard to national treatment. Myths inculcated by sustained propaganda remain, however, difficult to eradicate.

It is understandable that many in Nepal may feel that the 1950 treaty is a vestige of the Rana regime and, therefore, ipso facto unacceptable. What they may also soberly reflect upon is that the only remaining operational parts of the treaty provide the legal cover for millions of their citizens earning their livelihoods in India.

The 1950 treaty does not encompass the sum of India-Nepal relations. Agreements and arrangements between India and Nepal go well beyond the treaty. There is, for instance, the agreement on the recruitment of Nepali nationals into the Indian Army, which predates Indian Independence. A decision of the Indian Home ministry permits Nepali nationals to enter Indian government service. There is the open border between the two countries, permitting free movement. Other notable agreements include the Nepali rupee being tied to the value of the Indian rupee, as well as the interchangeability of the respective currencies. There are also agreements on water and hydroelectric resources, as also agreements on trade and transit. Indian development assistance to Nepal is still substantial, even if it is not proportionately as large as it was a few decades ago. Nepal's trade with India, Indian investments in Nepal and tourists from India are each of considerable substance, and indeed constitute the single largest volume in each category.

The presence of Nepali citizens, referred to as Gorkhas, in the Indian army is one of the unique features of Indo-Nepal relations and creates special bonds. The induction of Gorkhas into the British Indian Army served a particular purpose for British imperialism in India. Besides their famed valour in combat, they were also useful against Indian nationalists. As records reveal, their continuation in the army of an independent India was not a certainty as there were reservations about their record against Indian nationalists. The system was, however, continued, presumably partly out of respect for traditions prevalent in the army, as a means of indirect economic assistance and to retain existing bonds. It has been retained at the expense of several tens of thousands of Indian nationals who would otherwise fill these posts. It is an arrangement with which the 'Gorkhas' do not seem to have any problem and they were less than appreciative of the Maoist efforts to terminate their recruitment. The

Indian army and government seem willing to continue with the present arrangement. Recruitment of 'Gorkhas' in the Indian armed forces cannot take place without the consent of the Nepali government.

At the Foreign Office level discussions in 2001, the Nepali side had suggested that the deployment of the Gorkhas should be intimated to the Government of Nepal. The Indians had candidly responded that they were willing to terminate future recruitment, but would not be able to share information on deployment or operational matters.

There are presently around 30,000 Nepali Gorkhas in the Indian army as also substantial numbers in para military forces. Over 110,000 pensioners are settled in Nepal and draw over rupees 1000 crores in pension. It is an arrangement, which has so far stood the test of time.

Gorkhas in the Indian army besides, there have been good relations between the two national armies. The Nepali Army, a proud and disciplined force, cannot be unaffected by the winds of change swirling in the country. The Royal Nepal Army had close bonds with the palace and a process of redefining its character must be under way. India should not take the Nepali army for granted and try to build on the goodwill that exists. India is helping in the modernisation of Nepal army. Joint exercises between the two Armies can be a way forward, which will synergise their efforts in counter-terrorism. So far, the Nepali army has conducted itself impeccably. Unstated, but understood, is the concern that if the political situation should become increasingly fraught, the army may feel encouraged to play a more pro-active role.

It is a reflection of the inadequacies in Indo-Nepal relations that even after decades, there is still little movement on the development of the water resources of Nepal. After the Koshi and Gandaki projects, the last over forty years ago, the only significant project has been the Tanakpur barrage. The Mahakali Treaty, signed with great expectations a decade ago, has made little progress in implementation. Essentially, a feeling has remained in Nepal, or has been fostered, that the earlier agreements were in some way detrimental to Nepal. Looking at the balance of benefits to each country, these feelings are debatable.

Equally, India's ability to communicate adequately in the vital question of water management, be it with Nepal or Bangladesh, needs improvement. The issue is far too important to be entrusted to rigid technological dogmas and requires serious and sustained diplomatic and political input. There needs to be open public discussion of issues involved to alleviate possible apprehensions as also highlight the costs of delay.

The Himalayan rivers arising in or transiting Nepal have a significant achievable hydro-electric potential of 45,000 MW. In addition, and of no lesser importance, is the possibility of controlling the flows of the rivers for both flood control in the rainy season and augmentation of flows during the dry season. The optimum development of this resource is of great importance to India and for even further lower riparian, Bangladesh. Obviously, any future development must take fully into account concerns about displacement and environmental effects. These are issues, which have come up constantly in debates on the development of India's internal water resources. They have to be meaningfully addressed and the future cannot be tied down to simple economic cost benefit calculations. In the case of storage dams, Nepal would be justified in seeking remuneration for flood control or augmentation benefits that may accrue to India or Bangladesh. It may be recalled that in the long drawn out negotiations with India on Farakka in the 70s, Bangladesh had consistently proposed the inclusion of Nepal for purposes of augmentation. However, though nearly three decades have passed since India withdrew its reservations to this modality, no progress is in evidence. The absence of openness and the constant politicisation of the issue in Nepal have stymied progress. There has been the unusual spectacle of the party supporting the Mahakali Treaty subsequently despatching its cadres to block field investigations.

One hopes that the future would see rapid and meaningful co-operation between India and Nepal for development of this constantly renewable source of energy and the potential of water resources in a holistic manner for the benefit of both. The answers to what needs to be done are well known to experts on both sides. What continues to be absent is the political will and the commitment to go ahead. Nepal is particularly sensitive to the question of the development of water resources, partly perhaps because it sees this as an area where it holds an upper-hand vis-à-vis India. We need to acknowledge that unlike the situation half a century ago, today Nepal does have a body of experts, who can be engaged in constructive discussions. Some of the certainties that would have motivated, for instance, the construction of the Kosi barrage or the proposed Kosi high dam are now being questioned, reflecting divergences of view on the damming or training of rivers within India itself. Nepal must have greater sense of involvement and participation in future projects.

Recent positive developments have been the award of contracts for some hydro-electric projects. As far as India is concerned, there should be no reservations if Nepal chooses to enter into arrangements with third countries or parties for the development of its most significant resource. However, the cost benefit analysis of projects with an 'export' potential, be it power or water management, unavoidably brings in the Indian market. Clearly, India would not be able to commit to purchases if the costs are higher than what is domestically available, or economically feasible. These issues would need to be addressed. Nepal should not assume that India is dependent on Nepali development of its water resources. It should be seen as a commercial transaction, to be commercially negotiated.

Rivers do not understand political boundaries. Ideally, there should be a basin wise approach in considering long term programmes to maximize available resources to meet requirements. This also brings in China as about 20 per cent of the run off from Nepal is contributed by flows coming in from Tibet. Participation of China presently appears doubtful, but Bangladesh, India and Nepal could make an effort towards a holistic approach to water management. The countries involved have different perspectives and interests. India is the only one which is both a major upper as well as lower riparian. The absence of clear and binding international laws on water sharing or development does not make the task any easier.

In recent years, there have been comments in Nepal suggesting that Nepal has been losing time and money in not developing water resources and the example of Bhutan's fruitful co-operation with India has been quoted. There is thus some body of opinion favouring co-operation with India, which could be sensitively cultivated. Our first option for the future should be to offer Nepal generous terms for the utilization of its water resources, not only for power, but for flood control and dry season augmentation.

To avoid any future misunderstanding, it would be necessary to proceed on future agreements with complete transparency, ensuring that Nepal's civil society is always fully on board with regard to the implications of proposed movement as also the consequences of non-action. With Nepal presently undergoing massive power cuts, there should be a better grasp of the consequences of decades wasted.

As we look to the future of Indo-Nepal relations, it may be useful to glimpse the past.

In the early years, one discerns almost a sense of bewilderment in Jawaharlal Nehru's sense of frustration at Nepali actions and reactions on various issues. This was also accompanied at times by a tone of stern advice, which would have been more appropriate if administered to a state of the Indian Union, surprising though this might seem in view of his inherent and unflagging commitment to Nepali sovereignty. But if Nehru considered himself qualified to give such advice, over the years, Indian policy and policy makers were far too greatly influenced by the political and traditional elite of Kathmandu. Consequently, there has been a tendency for state to state relations being conducted at a highly personalized level and decisions at times hostage to personal equations. This has not benefited the state or the people of India and, it may be argued, has also not brought the benefits of co-operation with India to the Nepali people to the extent that may have been possible. And this is odd because it was Indian assistance in diverse fields including roads, airports and hospitals that helped Nepal enter the 20th century after having been fettered to an earlier age by the Rana rulers. Jawaharlal Nehru had uttered words of caution in describing pitfalls in Indo-Nepal relations, "Personalities count and must continue to count, but problems should not be considered in terms of personalities only, otherwise they would be reduced to the level of personal intrigues." Wise and prescient words that have not been heeded by either Nepal or India.

The degree of subjective assessments of a Nepal policy can be seen in the debates in India after the palace coup of 2005, shades of which still remain. It was strongly urged that the Royal Nepal Army was an institution friendly to India and must not be thwarted. The reality that the RNA was in a patently anti-people role and was collaborating with a king set on establishing an absolutist monarchy was simply ignored. Here is one instance, perhaps, where contrary to general principles, institutional connections between countries can cloud a larger vision about what is good for people as a whole rather than for segments.

And one may also recall here that even in the early sixties, right wing and feudal elements in India had urged support for Mahendra's step back in time. It has been recently claimed that he had been invited by a prominent Indian leader of the time to become the emperor of Hindu India.

It is customary to look upon Nepal as a part of South Asia. While this is geographically correct, the peoples have had different growth charts. It is necessary to recall that in colonized South Asia, a substantial middle class had developed from the 19th century, imbued with modern education and values. This was not so in Nepal where the effort was to ensure that the feudal order was perpetuated and where an active professional class has started to emerge only in the past half century. It is creditable that despite setbacks civil society in Nepal is showing great courage as one may observe in contemporary Nepali media. They could also play a vital role in future Indo-Nepal relations.

Any policies that India may pursue towards Nepal must first attempt an appreciation of Nepali concerns vis-a-vis India. While India may consider some to be unfounded, even as perceptions they need to be taken note of for future development of relations.

There is the overarching reality of Nepal's dependence on India. This is neither of India's choosing, nor Nepal's, but the outcome of history, geography and sheer economic compulsions. It is understandable that Nepal should try to find 'breathing space' and this is perhaps something that should be encouraged for the development of a healthy Nepali polity, free of undue angst. It was, in retrospect, unwise of India to have been indifferent to Birendra's proposal of Nepal as a Zone of Peace. It would not have made any difference to India's standing or influence in Nepal, while affording them an identity away from the yam, as pithily put by the founder of the nation. The fact is that nations react in much the same way as individuals, and dependence on India — imports, exports, transit, tourism etc. — is bound to breed resentment. If there are long queues at petrol stations, it is inevitable that it is the Indian Oil Corporation which would be held responsible for curtailing supplies, and not the Nepali importer, which has failed to clear long-standing dues.

And if Nepal is conscious and resentful of dependence on India, the often patronising Indian attitude does not help.

There is understanding and appreciation of the depth of religio-cultural links. But this also leads to fear of being assimilated. Such apprehensions are accentuated when Indians speak of unique or extraordinary relationships with Nepal as a Hindu kingdom. With a secular republican state in Nepal, this aspect will have lesser play.

Following calculated anti-Indian propaganda by the palace, and indoctrination by the communists, from the sixties, there is a belief that the treaties/agreements between Nepal and India are in some way 'unequal' and not conducive to Nepal's interests. This feeling has been internalised and used for political purposes by political parties in Nepal. Should the need arise, India should have no hesitation in agreeing to look at all treaties afresh, also underlining that in such a venture, each country would have to look to its own interests.

The large Indian share in Nepal's trade, tourism and investment is used by interested parties to promote apprehensions about Indian intentions. Negative views about India are held largely by parties commercially affected and are most prevalent in the Valley. While there is understanding of the employment opportunities available in India, which are crucial for Nepal's economy, this is taken for granted.

There is acute consciousness of dependence on India for links with outside world. This, in turn, breeds resentment and a desire to multiply links with Tibet as an alternative.

Public statements of preferences in Nepali politics, or denigration of developments, as sometimes voiced both by the Indian establishment and major Indian political parties, only confirm Nepal's worst fears about Indian intrusiveness in their affairs.

It is believed, with justification, that India influences political developments in Nepal. The 12 point peace accord is a major example of India acting as a facilitator. What is ignored is that Indian assistance/ advice is not imposed, but follows Nepali requests.

While taking note of Nepali reservations, one must not underestimate the many positives, tangible and intangible, that operate to India's advantage.

Cultural and familial connectivities form a deep bond between the peoples of the two countries. The ties between *madhesis* and their southern neighbours are significant and will remain so even as they acquire a greater say in the affairs of the state. The large number of retired Gorkha soldiers in the country, including in remote regions, have a positive attitude towards India.

Despite competition, business and industry in Nepal is fully cognisant of the need for maintaining and developing close links with India. They are beneficiaries of the unilateral duty free access afforded to Nepali goods. India is the natural source of investment in Nepal and this would be beneficial to Nepali partners.

As a landlocked country, access to the outside word is of obvious importance to Nepal. India's decision in the 80s to restrict such access to what might be required under international law (by no means a blockade as depicted) has left bitter memories. It can be argued that the incident did convey the message that Indian goodwill cannot be taken for granted and needs reciprocity, particularly in matters of concern to India. Though road links with China are being developed, and rail links may follow, these cannot replace the locational advantage enjoyed by India. Since resuming comprehensive transit facilities, India has also agreed to Nepal's transit links with Bangladesh and provided infrastructural assistance to facilitate movement of goods to and from Nepal. Geography shall continue to remain to India's advantage on this issue.

Nepal is in the process of far-reaching transition from a system and government of the few in the Valley to an inclusive polity, which will perforce have to reflect the interests of people hitherto on the fringes. Existing players will surely remain, but as surely new players would emerge on the political chessboard. Even the full contours of the changes that could or will take place cannot be discerned at the current period of flux. Whether this 'revolution', the first of its kind in South Asia, takes place smoothly or stumbles along the way, cannot yet be forecast. There are signs of erstwhile major political parties being uncomfortable with impending changes. But this could be largely the wishes of ageing leadership. It is likely that younger elements in such parties would be increasingly impatient if change is thwarted. The Maoists have become a house divided. Whichever way things work out, it would be an arduous journey for all stakeholders in Nepal. It is evident to the Nepalis that the "huzoor" mentality, carefully nurtured in feudal times, no longer exists. *chakari* is no longer an assured passport to prosperity. This also needs due recognition in India.

The desire for change in Nepal provides India an opportunity of recasting the substance of Indo-Nepal relations in a fresh mould. The substance and the content of the relations have never been in any doubt. But the approach would have contributed to many bottlenecks and the failure to realize the full potential. The following areas would need attention and appropriate pursuit:

It is well known that influential elements in the machinery of the Indian state as also in the army and others were supportive of the continuation of the monarchy, in some form at least, until developments in Nepal made this no longer possible. An erstwhile ruling party in India publicly displayed distress at the end of the Hindu monarchy. It is important that there are no mixed signals, at least from anyone associated with the Indian government, that India understands the Nepali people's desire for change and stands fully behind them. The manner of projection of this approach is no less important. We should not be, or seen to be, supportive of any political party or formation. This would also require us to be fine-tuned to the under-currents of people's expectations in Nepal.

India was the first country to provide substantial infrastructural aid to Nepal. While the share of Indian assistance relative to global assistance to Nepal has understandably diminished, it is still among the largest. Nepal's dependence on external assistance will continue for some time.

Given the importance of Nepal to India's security, in both conventional and non-conventional terms, it is time for us to consider substantially increasing the quantum of assistance. It may be noted that what India is offering Nepal today is a fraction of what is being invested in Afghanistan. Clearly, there would be questions of Nepal's ability to absorb aid, more so in these disturbed times. But both medium and long term plans should be drawn up for the development of infrastructure. Road building to less accessible areas should be a priority for this would impact visibly and positively on the lives of the people.

Equally, it is important to spread out widely in the countryside in small but visibly useful projects (bridges, culverts, hospitals, schools, cold storage units, drinking water, etc.), which can bring immediate and visible relief to people. India's efforts in this direction in recent years, with the stakeholders being responsible for the management of the projects, have been appreciated both by the people and their representatives. Its scope needs to be expanded.

Nepal's nearly eighteen hundred kilometre border abuts five Indian states — Uttarakhand, Uttar Pradesh, Bihar, Sikkim and West Bengal. There could be a range of issues or differences, as entirely possible between two neighbouring areas. In the case of a foreign country, it assumes greater importance and can lead to high decibel levels in the media — as, for instance, was seen with regard to the Laxmanpur barrage in Uttar Pradesh some years ago. Criminals from either country seeking refuge in the other is a perennial issue. Regular communications between the relevant authorities on either side of the border is necessary to prevent any issue from assuming larger than life dimensions. Delhi needs to evolve a mechanism of keeping in touch with the governments of the bordering Indian states to keep a watch on possible areas of difference, as also keep them sensitized about India's larger foreign policy interests.

One of India's principal objectives should be the creation and strengthening of economic linkages, thus creating an increasing body of stakeholders in Nepal for stable and predictable relations with India. India's aid, as well as economic and trade policies towards Nepal need to reflect this. There is a paradox of dependence reflected in Indo-Nepal relations. The present perception of dependence creates resentment. Yet, Indian aid and trade, tourism and investment remain crucial for Nepal. India's long term aim should be cooperation leading to a self reliant and economically vibrant Nepal. This, in turn, would facilitate the emergence of a self confident Nepali nationalism, no longer requiring the prop of anti-Indianism for the national psyche.

Regulation of the border is essential. This can be done only after the two countries mutually identify the present problems and decide on correctional steps. There are security issues on both sides. For India, it could be ISI activities or the smuggling of currency. Nepal would have concerns about cross-border activities or co-ordination of criminal elements. Clearly, open border cannot continue to denote unregulated border. One way forward could be to have integrated border development programmes. Besides bringing greater prosperity, it would give local residents an active stake and interest to see that undesirable activities do not take place. There would be human issues involved in greater regulation and the effort has to be to cause the least disturbance to links between peoples while ensuring a larger quantum of security. India may also consider discussing with Nepal a time-bound plan for regional development of the *terai* and an equal adjoining area of India in Bihar and UP.

With greater openings available both within and outside the country, the number of Nepali students studying in India would appear to be on the decline. It would be in India's long term interest if Nepali students do pursue studies in India. The fee structure for Nepali students and what additional facilities could reasonably be provided should be assessed.

Kathmandu has an age old tradition of pervasive suspicion and conspiratorial politics commented upon by a British Resident as far back as the 30s of the nineteenth century and many later analysts. Things are often not what they seem and even when so, are assumed to be otherwise. This can be of benefit to the class of self appointed intermediaries adept at representing, or misrepresenting, their principals. What can suffer as a consequence is the substance of inter-state relations. With regard to India, there are a host of carefully propagated misperceptions, be it with regard to treaties or development of water resources. A genuinely nationalist Nepali civil society and media (as against those, who equate Nepali nationalism with an anti-Indian posture) is in evidence with the emergence of a genuine middle class in Nepal. We are likely to see greater number of Nepali nationalists, who may judge issues on merits rather than be unduly influenced by pre-conceived notions. They should be India's natural allies in developing a wholesome relationship with Nepal.

If even as a postscript to Indo-Nepal relations, it is necessary to take a look at Nepal's relations with China because, at times, this threatens to adversely affect the former. A brief historical perspective is useful.

The founder of the Nepali state, Prithvi Narayan Shah, had remarked that Nepal was like a yam between two boulders. This was ingrained in Nepali decision makers and Nepal has tried ever since, not always successfully, to keep both boulders at bay by deft diplomacy. Facing the possibility of dire action by China after its own repeated invasions of Tibet, Nepal concluded a treaty of commerce with the East India Company in March, 1792, in the hope of deterring the Chinese. This did not help and as the Chinese forces approached Kathmandu, Nepal was compelled by the treaty of October, 1792 to cede territory south of the Himalayan watershed and to agree to what amounted to a quinquennial tribute, couched in polite terms, which was to continue till the early 20th century. As the eminent scholar and diplomat Rishikesh Shaha, puts it, "… But Nepal cooled off after being forced to sue for peace with China in October, 1792… British Parliament's criticism of subsidiary Alliances prevented the Governor General from pursuing similar approach towards Nepal" *(Rishikesh Shaha, NEPALI POLITICS Retrospect and Prospect, Oxford University Press 1978).*

The 1792 treaty with China stipulated (article 5) "that if Nepal be ever invaded by a foreign power, China would not fail to help her," but this was of no avail in the war leading to the Treaty of Sugauli. Shaha's broad sweep on the subject is instructive, "When Nepal found itself at war with the East India Company in 1814, it appealed unsuccessfully to China for military assistance — at the same time telling the Chinese that if they exerted too much pressure, then Nepal may turn to the British........ Although the Gorkhali skill in diplomacy and on the battlefield made a lasting impression on the Chinese, the war engendered in the minds of the Chinese officials in Tibet a sustained basic distrust of Nepali intentions. This kind of attitude was responsible for the failure of every attempt by the Nepalis to involve the Chinese in countering British expansions in India..... As a consequence, in the decades following the 1791-92 war, Nepal played a losing game in its efforts to balance the Chinese against the British in India. China paid little or no heed to Nepal's offers of help and requests of assistance during the first half of the 19th century. .... During the period before 1846, however, Nepal's pretensions of vassalage to China helped deter the British from absorbing the buffer state of Nepal into the British empire in India...... even Chandra Shamsher, who later as prime minister (1901-1929) became the greatest ally and friend of the British, was reported to have said openly to the British envoy as late as 1890 that since Nepal was subordinate to China, it could in no way be subordinate to the British Government of India" *(Shaha, Ibid.)*. Shaha makes the significant comment ".... but while China is judged by its overt actions, India is judged more by its externally projected psychological image. What Nepal thinks India is doing is more important than what India actually does." *(Shaha, Ibid.)*.

The China 'card' continued to be attempted by both royalists and, later, Maoists. King Mahendra did so, emboldened particularly after the Indian defeat in the border war of 1962. His instructions at the time reveal the intent of developing close relations with China. The internal politics of Nepal played a part. India's support to democratic forces would not have been pleasing to the palace. Dependence on India was galling and thoughts of a countervailing friendly China was attractive to the royalists. The then chief of the Royal Nepal Army had said to me in 2000 that Nepal's relations with India and China could be said to be in the ratio of 60:40. China as an option to India has been a running theme in Nepali strategic thinking, even if never fully developed. The Chinese themselves were pragmatic in their responses to Nepali overtures. Speaking to the high level Nepali delegation visiting Beijing on the occasion of the 25th anniversary of the communist revolution, Mao advised that Nepal should not concern itself with Sino-Indian differences. These were two great countries, who would sort out their problems. Nepal, Mao said, should concentrate on development and try to maintain good relations with India (In conversation with former Prime Minister Surya Bahadur Thapa).

Many years later, after accession to governance in 2008, Maoists looked for stronger ties with China. India had studiously ignored Prachanda's first visit abroad to Beijing (on the occasion of the Olympics) and had accorded him an extraordinarily warm welcome on his subsequent visit to Delhi in September 2008. In the following months, however, there were a flurry of high level and military exchanges between Kathmandu and Beijing. This would have been disturbing to Delhi. According to an analyst, "By April 2009, misgivings in New Delhi about the Maoists' close ties to China (especially the fraternal ties developing between the People's Liberation Armies in the two countries and Chinese commitment of military aid were giving way to alarm. High-level visits to Kathmandu by Chinese generals and discreet visits to Tibet by Maoist Defence Minister Ram Bahadur Thapa and Information Minister Krishna Bahadur Mahara convinced the Indians that the Maoists were collaborating with the Chinese to establish a totalitarian people's republic" *(Kunda Dixit, A New Himalayan Game).*

The Chinese, looking for stability in Nepal advised the Maoists to mend fences with India, as Mao had done some thirty years earlier. Maoists were advised to appreciate that there are two sides to a mountain, and Nepal should understand which side they are on.

There were contradictions in the relations between the Maoists and China. Any reading that the Maoists taking their name from the great Chinese revolutionary brings them close to Beijing would be shallow, even more so as Mao in China today would feel like Rip van Winkle. Given the indoctrination about Indian expansionists, it has not been difficult for the Maoists to attempt a Chinese embrace. The fact of China being among the very few countries supportive of Gyanendra's coup of 2005, and possibly the only one to supply arms at the time to the Royal Nepal Army to fight the Maoist insurgency, is not remembered. It is also not widely known that in the days of insurgency, Maoists who had gone across the border to seek arms assistance from China were detained.

There was, at the time, a suspicion in Beijing that the Maoists were being supported by India. It was a misreading of India's intentions to support democratic forces with the allied effort to bring the Maoists into the political mainstream.

But the apparent contradiction is resolved if it is seen in the context of the essence of Chinese policy towards Nepal. China may be willing to play low cost games in Nepal to frustrate India, but India is not the primary focus of their attention. Primary Chinese concern in Nepal is the establishment of a strong central authority, regardless of its political hue, who can deliver on Chinese security interests in Tibet. Hence their traditional links with the palace and, in particular, support to Gyanendra when he was mistakenly thought to be in control. Hence, also their high profile wooing of the Maoists after their remarkable showing in the elections.

Having pursued their objectives through the palace for several decades, the Chinese now have to face the dilemma of dealing with a democratic Nepal. This would, at least partially, explain their reaching out to a broad spectrum of political parties and the focus on cultural activities, such as the opening of study centres.

If the right and the left deliberately underline an exaggerated policy of friendship towards China, there is also a broad non-ideological consensus for enhancing ties with Beijing. China is a major international player with global reach and, quite understandably,

Nepal, a neighbour, would wish to benefit from closer co-operation. There was a fair amount of media attention to the connectivity between Syabrubeansi and Rasuagadi. (Rasuagadi as well as Zhangmu, which is connected by the Arniko highway, were ceded by Nepal to China after their defeat in 1792. Both are on the southern slopes of the Himalaya). There is rapid construction of the road from central Nepal along the Kali Gandaki, which would soon give access to Pokhara from Tibet. Also a road in eastern Nepal beyond Thaplejung. All these were decided upon years ago, even during the rule of the Nepali Congress and the UML. They reflect a broad desire in Nepal for greater connectivity with Tibet.

India and China have one common interest in Nepal. Each for its own reasons would like political stability. China would, in addition, prefer a strong central government whose writ may run across the nation. China is indifferent to the form of governance in Nepal, though judging by its own system and its past and present friends, may be more comfortable with autocratic regimes. China is happiest with state to state relations, but would, if it has to, engage with the people, as demonstrated by their recent displays of energy. The welfare of the Nepali people is of no direct interest to China. For India, on the other hand, both democracy and the welfare of the Nepali people are of direct and abiding interest.

Conclusion

Despite the promises held out by the people's movement of 2006, and notwithstanding the ability of the political parties to step back from the brink at critical times, the future remains uncertain. Nepal has awaited a constitution — freely arrived at and not handed down — for over six decades. "Hereafter, our subjects shall be governed by a democratic constitution to be framed by a constituent assembly elected by the people," said King Tribhuvan as he assumed power after the exit of the Ranas. That promise has not been kept. The Constituent Assembly elected in 2008 amid great expectations ended in a midnight whimper. While one must hope for a better performance from the next CA, this would remain contingent on the political parties, displaying a greater sense of urgency and commitment to a secure future than immediate political gains.

Among the many important issues seeking resolution, not the least important is the question of federalism. Interests of different classes, castes and ethnic groups are pulling in different directions. The core issues of legitimate entitlement, from the *janjatis* or the *madhesis,* can no longer be left to hibernate. It is useful to quote here from Subba, "From the available literature, it appears that there is increasing concern among scholars of Nepal about the difficulty faced by many of its peoples, particularly those of hill ethnicity and the terai population in identifying themselves with the given Nepali national identity. The Tibeto-Burman hill communities have challenged the notion of "one nation, one dress, one language, one religion" propagated by Kathmandu officialdom, putting many mainstream scholars on the defensive about the history and sociology of Nepal. In short, the question of national identity has become one of the most contentious issues in the country *(Tanka Bahadur Subba, Nepal and the Indian Nepalis from State of Nepal, edited by Kanak Mani Dixit and Shastri Ramachandran, Himal Books, 2002).*

The issue of national identity faces a two pronged challenge. One, as pointed out by Subba, is the challenge from hitherto disadvantaged groups seeking their own identity in the sun. The other related issue is the very definition itself of what constitutes the Nepali nation and, hence, nationalism. To make a brief comparison with her neighbours, China is an ancient civilisation, but today, a Han centric empire where the states in the periphery are in various stages of discontent. India, too, is an ancient civilization and has been, above all, a concept stretching from the mountains to the sea long before it became a nation. Nepal, also, goes back many centuries. But this Nepal, both physically and conceptually, was confined to the valley of Kathmandu. Today's Nepal is the product of Gorkha conquests of the 18th century, with some subsequent adjustments. But the definition of Nepal continued to be centred on the valley even as the state of Nepal was identified with the monarch. It has been suggested that "only about 1909 was the country referred to as Nepal. Earlier 'Nepal' meant only the Valley and the other constituents as subject territories. ...... In the 1930s, Gorkha and Gorkhali were substituted by Nepal and Nepali." *(See Nationalism and Ethnicity in a Hindu Kingdom: Whelpton and Others, Harwood Academic Publishers, 1997).*

While the people of Nepal resided in the territory of Nepal, their sole loyalty was ordained to be to the person of the monarch. He was projected as lord Vishnu incarnate. The king was Nepal, even if he had been kept in golden fetters for a hundred years. As the monarchy revived, the only 'nationalism' inculcated in the people was the centrality of the king together with the negative one of anti-Indianism, as it sustained the monarch's self proclaimed role as the sole protector against Indian expansionism.

With the abolition of monarchy, Nepal would need to define a new 'nationalism'. The lead for this has to come from politicians, academics, cultural activists, musicians, poets and from civil society in general. The love for and commitment to the nation has to be inclusive. This, again, cannot be achieved unless the pending questions on federalism are resolved.

In keeping with the primacy of politics over all else as evidenced in Nepal, there is scant analysis of the huge economic costs suffered by the nation and its people in the years of turmoil and uncertainty, for which there is no accountability. With a population of some 28 million, nature has endowed Nepal with immense possibilities, which could make it the richest state in South Asia. Properly organized, tourism, now confined largely to the casinos in the cities or backpackers in the *himals,* could bring in multiples of the present revenues. Organised cultivation of precious herbs in the mid hills and meadows could change the lives of the local people, as was evidenced in the efforts of an Indian pharmaceutical company. I recall people carrying sackfulls of medicinal roots from the remote area of Rara Lake to be sold to the middlemen on the Indian border for a pittance. Properly cultivated and organised, they could be a huge foreign exchange earner. Industry and investment have retreated with the uncertainty of attacks by political cadres and the absence of government guidelines and decisions. Today, Nepal produces about two percent of its hydro electric potential and, ironically, seeks to import power from India. Its development alone would change the face of the nation. Besides export of energy, it would attract energy intensive industries for value addition and employment.

In this phase of transition, there is the possibility of latent anti-Indianism being nurtured as the basis of nationalism, drawing on the past policies of the palace, more recently demonstrated by the Maoists as well as others when it suits their immediate political ends. This can only be harmful to Nepal. As Kanak Mani Dixit puts it, "Realistically, Nepal cannot benefit when an ideology of ultra nationalism guides our powerful political parties. For the people of Nepal to benefit economically from all that the country can deliver, the key hurdle to surmount is the knee jerk anti-Indianism that is ignited at regular intervals. Nepal's spiteful ultra-nationalism has been based not on national pride or the search for sovereign equality with New Delhi, but on self serving personal agenda ... who care little that anti-Indian ultra-nationalism destroys prospects for investment, market openings and tourism, and undermines the security and the livelihood of Nepali citizens working in millions in India. The more ultra-nationalist Nepali society becomes, the more we will miss the investment of above-board businesses and multinationals and fall into the stranglehold of carpetbagger businessmen from India" *(Kanak Mani Dixit, Peace Politics of Nepal, Himal Books, 2011).*

"There is," writes Ruhi Tewari, *"something very disconcerting about the common Nepali's suspicion and in fact even mistrust and abhorrence towards India's role in the country. There is a belief in a certain section that India's sole purpose is to interfere in the internal affairs of Nepal so as to destabilize the country and that it spends all its time identifying strategies to do this." (Ruhi Tewari, The India Hangover, My Republica, July 2012).*

Responding to a fictitious account of a 'secret' visit to Kathmandu, Shyam Saran wrote, "As ambassador to Nepal from 2002 to 2004, I was struck by how a section of the Kathmandu political and civil society elite and media was convinced that the Indian government spent most of its waking hours figuring out how to subvert Nepal when the really big challenge was how to get enough attention for Nepal in New Delhi's political and bureaucratic establishment. If there is one industry, which is always flourishing in Nepal it is its fabled rumour mill, with its handlers vying with each other to produce the most imaginative and even bizarre stories about Indian activities in Nepal" *(Shyam Saran, "Kathmandu's Conspiracy Theorists," Indian Express, July, 2012).*

In my view, the anti-Indian sentiments referred to, whether they are genuine or manipulated for political objectives, are very largely confined to the Valley and do not permeate Nepal as a whole. Nevertheless, since Kathmandu is the seat of decision making, it requires due attention. It should also be noted that while there is no 'anti- Nepal' sentiment in India, there could be among decision makers and even among those with goodwill towards Nepal, occasional feeling of ennui in facing Nepali ultra-sensitivity. This cannot augur well for the future.

Given the large country, small country syndrome, exacerbated by Nepal's real and perceived dependence on India, it is not difficult to whip up anti-Indian sentiments. At the same time, in my travels through large areas of Nepal, as also interactions in Kathmandu, I have found funds of goodwill and regard for India and Indians. Thus, even if India may not aspire to winning popularity contests in Nepal, it should not assume either a permanent or widespread antipathy towards it.

A point made to me by some Nepali friends is that in its actions and reactions, India often does not distinguish between friends and those for whom anti-Indianism is a creed, either through inflexible political conviction or as a convenient tool to divert attention from their own shortcomings. Indian reaction to criticism can at times be sharp, but this would be misplaced when the criticism comes not from malice, but a nationalist Nepali perspective, even if prickly at times, on issues on which there can be genuine differences of opinion. On the other hand, there are those either with an in-built distaste towards India (to be found largely among former palace adherents) or politicians, who find India a soft target to enthuse their constituencies, as also some communists due to their indoctrination. I was advised that India should ensure that its views should be made known clearly to such classes or individuals. Detached indifference to their anti-Indian activities does not convey the right signals to the polity as a whole, least to those who feel that positive relations with India are in Nepal's interest.

Because of multiple points of contact and influence, it is difficult for India to pursue a wholly structured policy towards Nepal as vested interests on both sides would like to mould individual decisions to their own advantage. Granted that, there must needs be a focal point whose word shall be deemed to be final. The Ministry of External Affairs is the obvious choice and it should be able to handle skilfully both external as well as internal diplomacy in dealing with issues concerning Nepal. Even as some decisions are bound to be guided by exigencies of the time, it is critical to ensure that India's approach is always within the parameters of India's — and Nepal's — long term interests.

In the recent past, there have been occasions when India has appointed special envoys to convey messages from the highest levels. These visits have been linked to internal developments in Nepal. This procedure has doubtful advantages. Consultations between India and Nepal relating to political developments do take place, but the best channel for this is the Indian ambassador in Kathmandu. Visits by special envoys, particularly if they become routine, detract from the position of the ambassador as the accredited representative of India. Related to this is the practice, now possibly discontinued, of having interlocutors, outside normal diplomatic channels, as was in evidence with the palace. This had the twin disadvantage of confusing the elected representatives, even if this had not been India's intention, and the uncertainty of whether the designated intermediary was conveying messages to either side as actually received from the principals. Overall, these practices detract from the need for transparent state to state interactions, which is important to establish in Indo-Nepal relations.

In my discussions in Nepal across a wide cross section of eminent personalities who have had, and continue to have, interactions with India, as also observers of Indo-Nepal relations, there was one common refrain. That India's advice on internal issues was often the most useful and should continue to be provided. However, India needs to be meticulous in not attempting to micro-manage affairs. Impartial advice, once tendered, should be left to Nepali interlocutors to proceed further on their own, in their own best judgement. One might add that micro management does not promote or encourage confidence in handling one's own affairs or inculcating the habit of being responsible for the consequences of one's actions.

Also associated with this must be the manner in which Indians conduct themselves at various levels. A sensitive Nepali reaction was conveyed by a Nepali friend in my early days in Kathmandu. "We do understand, ambassador, that there are all kinds of things that you may be required to do. But please leave us our self respect."

As the internal churning continues in Nepal, India and Nepal must seriously adjust the manner of their political interactions. So far, there was a degree of comfort on both sides flowing from past associations. This will no longer be available to the same degree. It is likely that the new generation of leaders and activists in Nepal may come from different backgrounds, with little direct knowledge of India or the political and bureaucratic processes south of the border. There would be need to build mutual confidence and understanding in a 'language' both can understand and accept. India must avoid any condescension towards Nepal and be equally careful not to acquiesce in unreasonable demands. What India should seek to encourage at the political level is not just friendship, but mutual understanding of mutual interests. Friendship with political classes can be transient, and sometimes go to the highest bidder, but friendship among nations has to be built on national interests. Despite its 'uniqueness', Indo-Nepal relations fall within this paradigm.

The emergence of the Maoists as a significant political force may have changed the politics of Nepal irrevocably, even as their ideological rigidity diminishes further over time. They have — successfully — projected themselves as the torch bearer of long suppressed aspirations, qualitatively different from the traditional politics of Nepal. Their future success depends largely on the ability of traditional parties to respond to the challenges of popular aspirations.

There are strong views about the Maoists in Nepal. To quote Kanak Mani Dixit, "The Maoist agenda has been to foment chaos, destroy all institutions and due process, and be there to reap the fall out" (*Kanak Mani Dixit, Peace Politics of Nepal, Himal Books, 2011*) Statements emanating in the past from Maoist ideologues, concerns about the activities of the Youth Communist League and uncertainty about the future of the Maoist cadres, may prompt such reactions. But many have been overtaken by events and while in governance on two occasions, the Maoists have abided by their 2005 commitment to a multi-party democracy. There could be serious national problems in the future if core national issues (including the framing of the long awaited constitution) are not addressed. But the responsibility for this would have to be borne not by the Maoists alone. All stakeholders would need to recognize that a Pandora's box of expectations has been opened and it would not be possible to put the genie back and seal the box. Further, scope for fragmented but violent resistance in the countryside, whether in the hills or the *terai*, should be reduced.

The conservative Indian establishment had taken a leap of faith in supporting the agreement between the Nepali political parties and the Maoists, facilitating their soft landing in a democratic framework. But Maoist miscalculations vis-a-vis China and, finally, reneging on their commitment not to interfere with the military, brought about a change in Indian attitudes. But that India was willing to deal positively with a Maoist government committed to principles agreed to, both internally and externally, was demonstrated by her positive approach to the government headed later by Baburam Bhattarai. This approach of dealing with governments in Nepal without prior prejudice must continue.

For India, an allied challenge would be to cultivate the future federated units and their local leadership. The new provinces would become increasingly important and require individual attention, both politically and economically. India, like the policy makers of Kathmandu, would have to deal with grassroots politicians and the basic requirements of the people to whom its economic assistance would need to be targeted.

Despite its landlocked status, Nepal has considerable geo-political advantages, inadequately appreciated abroad and less in Nepal itself. Nepal has a significant location south of the soft underbelly of China and north of the open Indian plains. Both have perceptions of security vulnerability, and both would follow keenly internal developments in Nepal and try to ensure that their security concerns are not jeopardized. It would require both wisdom and tact on the part of Nepal that neither feels insecure. The past games of trying to prey on the insecurities of neighbours had never quite succeeded, and may today have more serious consequences.

With two large markets on either side, Nepal is ideally placed to attract international establishments and investments. In a negation of Prithvinarayan Shah's gloomy prognosis, both India and China have a vested interest in a stable Nepal, and hence its welfare. Nor does either have territorial claims. But to parlay its inherent advantages to positive gains, Nepal would need a coherent policy built on a self assured polity. And the development of its hydro-electric potential can give it a wealth and status that would be unimaginable today.

In its relationship with Nepal, India must make a distinction between its core interests and those of a more ephemeral nature. Development of water resources is important, but is not of core interest to India (as, indeed, it should be to Nepal for sheer economic reasons) as other options are open to her. Security is of primary and core interest and requires constant monitoring and interaction.

The nearly 1800 km open border, of which close to 1600 kms are in the open terai, poses obvious security concerns. It has been consistently misused by Pakistan. Is policing the border a viable option? Does Nepal need to be more involved with and concerned about the misuse of the border against Indian interests? Has India shown sufficient sensibility to Nepali concerns about criminal elements with trans-border activities? It would be useful if India and Nepal could draw up a charter of responsibilities for the management of the border to protect the interests of each. The two countries need to jointly patrol the border to check trans-border criminal activities, transfer of arms, human trafficking, etc. Like India, Nepal also faces the problem of criminals crossing the border and taking refuge in India and this issue cannot be addressed without joint management of the border.

Border management has been talked about, but not much progress seems to be visible. Even the check-posts on the Indian side have not seen much improvement and remain a dismal introduction to India. The open border regime should not be changed. But adequate steps are required both for ensuring security and to remove cause for legitimate complaints. One suggestion that has not been followed up is for focused development in the border areas on both sides. India needs to pursue on a priority basis the establishment of integrated check posts and provision of support facilities, which are presently inadequate. The state of the border check-posts continues to be a sad commentary on our neighbourhood focus and a poor introduction to India for visitors.

In the past, there have been occasions when the government of Nepal have not taken adequate notice of the mischief carried out against India from within its borders by third countries. This was noticeable after the 1999 hijacking of the Indian Airlines flight from

Kathmandu, to which India had reacted sharply. Recent trends are positive and the arrest of some high profile Indian terrorists from Nepal is a welcome indication of the co-operation between the two countries on security related issues.

India can be firm and unequivocal about its *lakshman-rekhas* only when there is a consensus on where this lies. There is presently inadequate clarity on this. Because of the multiplicity of points of interaction with Nepal, it is not always clear to the Nepalis what our sensitivities are.

Core interests have to be differentiated from involvement in Nepal's internal politics, which is often encouraged by Nepali parties or individuals for their own interests. India's national interests cannot be met if it is seen to be against the tide of opinion and expectations in Nepal. India had come close to the brink of a major error in implied support for Gyanendra during *jana andolan II* in April, 2006. There is need to play by a different set of rules based on transparency, which only can neutralise some of the misperceptions about India, which have been deliberately cultivated. In the foreseeable future, India will not be able to disengage from the dynamics of Nepal's internal politics and politicians and civil society across a wide spectrum not infrequently seek India's assistance in untying knots. But this must not be allowed to be the main focus. Indian policy makers also need to bear in mind Jawaharlal Nehru's remarks in this respect over six decades ago (*see Introduction).* It also needs to be borne in mind that statements emanating from responsible quarters in India are taken seriously in Nepal. Hence, there is need for studied sobriety in any public comments on developments in Nepal. This is particularly applicable to the expression of preferences with regard to political parties in Nepal.

China will continue to be a factor in Indo-Nepal relations. Traditionally, China has not been pro-active in Nepal. But this may be changing for a variety of reasons. Besides concerns about Tibet and a reflection of China's assertive policies elsewhere in the region, there would also be the need to adjust to a multi-polar federal Nepal where a cosy relationship with Kathmandu alone would not be adequate.

Recently, former prime minister and chairman of the UCPN (Maoist), Pushpa Kamal Dahal, has floated the idea of India and China co-operating and collaborating in the development of Nepal. As prime minister, Baburam Bhattarai had also suggested the possibility of Nepal being a vibrant bridge between India and China.

The Chinese response has been diplomatic, while India has been lukewarm. It is certainly an idea with possibilities which should not be merely noted and shelved, even if it may not become feasible until India and China develop a greater degree of mutual trust. It is arguably a contemporary version of king Birendra's idea of Nepal as a zone of peace. If the two boulders on either side of Nepal decide to co-operate, they are not likely to squeeze Nepal. Whatever the eventual fate of the proposal, it is important for India and China to remain in touch with regard to developments in Nepal. They may not agree on all aspects, but certainly share a desire for internal stability in Nepal. Their common perception is reflected in both stressing the importance of elections in Nepal at the earliest. It is a season of change in Sino-Nepal relations as the former reaches out to people rather than, as in the past, limiting themselves to purveyors of power. This is legitimate activity. But if Chinese activism in Nepal is perceived by India as unacceptably detrimental to its interests, this could lead to a spiral of unintended consequences.

A complicating factor here is Chinese apprehensions about western powers using Nepal against its interests in Tibet. One area of concern is the large numbers of conversions to Christianity in recent years and foreign missionary or NGO activities, which are presumed to be sympathetic to western interests. A greater concern is with regard to the activities of Tibetan refugees. Nepal is not the Nepal of the 50s or the 60s, and will not allow anti-Chinese activities from its soil. At the same time, it stands to lose western sympathies on whose assistance it remains dependent, should it adopt harsh measures against Tibetan refugees. In recent years, different governments of Nepal appear to have shown greater sensitivity to China's real or perceived concerns on this issue than basic considerations of human rights.

As the Chinese footprint increases in Nepal, India would have to see that the pursuit of Chinese interests do not impinge on India's security interests. Redlines on this would need to be considered and drawn and conveyed to the Nepali establishment. India would also need to be in communication with the United States and the west so that they do not take any steps in Nepal, which could upset the balance and lead to greater Chinese assertiveness and, consequently, India's inevitable negative responses. India and Nepal would also need to develop a mechanism through which collateral damage to their bilateral relations through third country activities is avoided.

It may be expected that as in the past two centuries, elements in Nepal would like to flaunt the China card from time to time, both as a measure of self assurance as also to convey to India that it has other options. Indian reaction would need to be measured, ensuring that facts are sifted from fiction and its response is guided only by considerations of its own interests, also appreciating that Nepal has an intrinsic right to parlay its geographical location and proximity to a great power to its own economic advantage. So far, the essence of China's advice to Nepal has been to act in recognition of their geographical situation and maintain good relations with India. But there is a long history of Nepali miscalculation on this issue, most recently demonstrated by the Maoists after accession to power in 2008. Nor can one rule out the Chinese adopting a more aggressively intrusive posture in the future. Their public opposition to federalism is a departure from the past.

Cooperation in management and development of water resources is a perennial issue. In the long term, optimum development of the waters of the Ganga basin requires involvement of all three countries concerned — Nepal, Bangladesh and India. In the current political scenario in Nepal, we cannot expect much forward movement in mega projects. However, Nepal and India, particularly UP and Bihar, must be in regular contact to ensure that irritants with reference to issues such as embankments are not allowed to fester. Cross border exchange of information, either by ground observation or satellite imagery should be formalised to create confidence. In discussions with civil society, India should convey that it would welcome co-operation with Nepal and the possible association of Bangladesh in future projects. This is not, however, a make or break issue with

India. It is for Nepal to determine what is of advantage to them as well as the timing. India would also need to look at the issue from the perspective of what is best suited to its interests. I recall a senior official of the Indian water establishment telling me in the context of no movement on the Mahakali treaty that since Nepal appeared to have no confidence in Indian intentions, it would be best for India not to consider future investments in Nepal in this sector and focus instead entirely on possibilities in India itself. Such an approach may be self-defeating, but can get greater traction if there is no progress on agreed areas.

Civil society of Nepal has come of age in the past decade. In fact, it may play an increasingly significant role given the political contestations of the day. India would need to make sustained efforts at encouraging interactions with Nepali interlocutors where Indian perspectives could be conveyed and Nepali perspectives understood. This would be of importance on the full spectrum of relations, particularly those, which have acquired negative connotations, such as the 1950 Treaty or water resources.

Presently, Nepal is attempting to negotiate its way through a labyrinth of long standing issues of visceral importance seeking resolution. It is an arduous process. As a country with prime stakes in the unity and stability of Nepal, India would observe developments with the keenest interest. As a friend, it should extend any helping hand that may be required and sought.

Postscript

Since the previous chapters were completed in mid-2013, political activity has remained centre stage in Nepal, even if developments, measured in terms of progress to a definable goal, have continued to be slow.

The results of the 2008 elections to the Constituent Assembly had been unexpected for both winners and losers, with an endorsement of the Maoists and a stern caution to the established political parties. With the failure of the assembly to deliver a constitution, fresh elections were held in November, 2013, with equally unforeseen results. This time, the Maoists were at the receiving end of the nation's disappointment while the traditional parties regained much lost ground.

The steep fall and rise in respective vote shares in the 2013 elections, in both the directly elected and proportional segments, saw the Maoist share of the 575 elected seats in the assembly fall by nearly two thirds from 229 to 80, while the Nepali Congress improved from 115 to 196 and the UML from 108 to 175. Significantly, the latter two with their share of nominated members, besides some outside assistance, would cross the critical two-thirds majority required for framing a new constitution. While the fortunes of the *madhes* based parties dipped, the Rashtriya Prajatantra Party, seen to represent the interests of the erstwhile monarchy, tripled its seats to 24 through the PR route.

Following a political understanding on the sharing of power, the Nepali Congress and the UML have been in governance under Sushil Koirala of the NC. A common decision to arrive at a draft constitution by January 22, 2015, has not fructified. There are pressures from within the coalition to frame a constitution on the strength of its two-thirds majority in the assembly, driven largely by the UML, which expects to occupy the prime ministerial chair when a constitution is in place. Outnumbered in the assembly, the Maoists and the *madhes* based parties want the spirit of consensus to prevail in the framing of the constitution. In their view, a majoritarian constitution will negate the spirit of the peace accords of the past. The Maoists continue to express their commitment to a peaceful resolution, though there are voices that suggest a violent response if there is a constitution that does not address the long standing aspirations of the people. Others apprehend a state of anarchy or even a renewed interest in a revived monarchy, however far-fetched this may appear. Polarization between opposing points of view seems to have hardened, even as the populace must be wondering at the inability of their elected representatives to come to some understanding.

There are no fresh issues thrown up in the current impasse. Following the explosion in *madhes* in January, 2007, there had been consensus that Nepal would constitute a federal republic. The *janjatis* have also seen in this the emancipation from their past issues of non-inclusion. While there is no going back on the principle of federalism, the contours of the new constituent units remain under dispute. The ruling coalition has cited economic viability for their preferences. Others feel that this would continue the control of the hill upper castes. There are, besides, differences within *madhes* on how the southern districts are to be configured.

During the extended term of the first constituent assembly (May 28, 2008 to May 28, 2012), there was no point in which a ruling coalition reflected consensus, which had been the basis of the seminal Delhi agreement of November, 2005, and the many subsequent agreements before the elections of 2008. It is also true; however, that the earlier spirit of consensus had been encouraged by the immediate challenges of the time and did not necessarily reflect a broader common vision of the future. The assembly, elected primarily to frame a constitution, acted largely as a parliament for governance, with parties vying for power, thus losing focus on the prime task at hand. The entirely infructuous debate on the induction of Maoist cadres into the Nepal army lost a very great deal of time. There had been no sense of urgency or desire to adhere to time tables.

The desire of the present ruling coalition to enact a constitution by virtue of its majority would signal a farewell to consensus. Equally, those bruised in the last elections have to accept that their numbers do not permit a result where all their wishes can be fulfilled. It may be simplistic, but not entirely inaccurate, to summarise that what continues to be played out are the differences between those, who look at issues through the prism of traditional governance and would like the least possible changes in existing systems, and others who claim to speak for those seeking fundamental attitudinal and structural changes, accommodating their quest for inclusion and autonomy. The legitimacy of the latter demands would need to be acknowledged and met in some form.

So far, the political parties have not distinguished themselves in the long drawn out debates. Deadlines have come and gone. The objective has been garnering presumed political capital. What has been absent is a vision of Nepal as it tries to emerge into a new era after centuries of feudal domination and exclusion.

Another major decision confronting the Constituent Assembly would be the chosen method of governance. Assuming that there would be an acceptable mixture between first-past-the-post and proportional representation, the issue of codifying the powers of the parliament, prime minister and president, still remains. Traditional parties may continue to feel comfortable with a Westminster type of undiluted parliamentary democracy, but Nepal's record of some twenty governments in twenty years does beg the question of stable governments. This acquires greater importance given that the earlier focus of Nepali nationhood, the palace, is no more. While there are no fissiparous tendencies in Nepal, differences between and among political parties, ranging from principles to personalities, have been endemic and a strong centre would be desirable, even as the new federated units enjoy their place in the sun. There are several models globally to choose from, and the Constituent Assembly should be able to find one, with modifications if necessary, to suit Nepal's unique requirements.

Besides core issues of the constitution, there is the continued demand for justice for those killed, maimed or raped by all sides during the years of insurgency. This has been understandably stonewalled by those involved, but the issue will not go away.

Even as intensive parlays continue in Kathmandu with regard to the future of constitution drafting, from India's point of view, it is a happy augury that she has not so far been charged, except by innuendos from the ultra sensitive, with interfering in domestic decision making. Credit for this is due to Prime Minister Narendra Modi.

The first Indian prime minister to undertake a bilateral visit to Nepal in 17 years, Mr Modi touched Nepali hearts by his candour and the ability to openly refer to subjects that have traditionally preyed on Nepali sensitivities without the slightest tinge of a patronizing attitude, regrettably common to Indians. Speaking as the head of the government of a sovereign state, he conveyed the respect due to another. With a liberal use of religious symbols, Modi underlined the many age-old bonds between the two nations.

Modi displayed a deft touch in dealing with sensitive issues. The contribution of the Gorkhas to Indian security was warmly acknowledged. On water resources, Nepal had to make its sovereign decision on how to proceed, beneficial as development would be for the nation.

The Indian prime minister hailed the end of violence in Nepal, an implicit but positive acknowledgement of the entry of the Maoists into a democratic framework. On the framing of the constitution, his comments laid out a vision of inclusiveness, where all communities could enjoy a sense of participation. Modi suggested that constitutions should unite, not divide and the weight of the present must not bury the hope for the future. He enjoined the members of the assembly to approach drafting of the constitution with the mind of the sages of the past, who built for the future generations. While the Nepali political classes and civil society had no hesitation in wooing Indian support during the last days of the rule by the palace a decade ago, some elements have chosen to be critical of Modi's sage advice, which was tendered without any specific formula on the steps to be taken.

Prime Minister Modi's approach to Nepal and Indo-Nepal relations has been welcomed by the people in general, the political classes, the media and civil society. His offers of assistance and cooperation in a variety of sectors, as also a concessional loan of 10,000 crore (NR), did not appear transactional, but as arising from a genuine desire for development in Nepal, as 'India feels cold when an adverse wind blows in Nepal'. Modi underlined that Indian advice, or material assistance would depend entirely on Nepal's sovereign decision to seek such involvement.

The success of Modi's visit to Nepal (and a subsequent one for the SAARC summit), also lies in the long hiatus since the previous bilateral visit of an Indian prime minister. It affirmed engagement at a political level and was a salve for sensibilities. It also raised hopes that henceforth the Indian political establishment would take a direct interest in Indo-Nepal relations. It would, however, be necessary for

India to ensure that any commitments made are fulfilled within schedules, as far as they lie with India.

Another, even if tangential, benefit of the Modi visit has been laying to rest apprehensions (or expectations, depending on one's point of view) that a BJP government in Delhi would be proactively supportive of Nepal's re-emergence as a Hindu state. This was evident even before the Indian elections in May, 2014, when a victory for the BJP seemed imminent. Though Modi certainly wore his personal Hindu credentials, he also noted that India respected and welcomed Nepal's emergence as a Federal Democratic Republic.

Even as relations with India are presently on an even keel, important national issues continue to be fiercely contested in Kathmandu. One can but hope that the wisdom displayed by political actors at critical times in the past will resurface to create a future of possibilities that the people of Nepal deserve and await.

Annexures

Annexure 1

Treaty of "Peace and Friendship" between the Government of India and the Government of Nepal, 31 July, 1950

The Government of India and the Government of Nepal recognizing the ancient ties which have happily existed between the two countries for centuries;

Desiring still further to strengthen and develop these ties and to perpetuate peace between the two countries;

Have resolved, therefore, to enter into a Treaty of Peace and Friendship with each other and have, for this purpose, appointed as their plenipotentiaries the following persons, namely, *The Government Of India, His Excellency Shri Chadreshwar Prasad Narain Singh*, Ambassador of India in Nepal; *The Government Of Nepal, Mohan Shamsher Jang Bahadur Rana*, Maharaja, Prime Minister and Supreme-Commander-in-Chief of Nepal, who having examined each other's credentials and found them good and in due form have agreed as follows:

Article 1

There shall be everlasting peace and friendship between the Government of India and the Government of Nepal. The two Governments agree mutually to acknowledge and respect the complete sovereignty, territorial integrity and independence of each other.

Article 2

The two Governments hereby undertake to inform each other of any serious friction or misunderstanding with any neighbouring State likely to cause any breach in the friendly relations subsisting between the two Governments.

Article 3

In order to establish and maintain the relations referred to in Article 1, the two Governments agree to continue diplomatic relations with each other by means of representatives with such staff as is necessary for the due performance of their functions.

The representatives and such of their staff as may be agreed upon shall enjoy such diplomatic privileges and immunities as are customarily granted by international law on a reciprocal basis:

Provided that in no case shall these be less than those granted to persons of a similar status of any other State having diplomatic relations with either Government.

Article 4

The two Governments agree to appoint Consuls-General, Consuls, vice-consuls and other consular agents, who shall reside in towns, ports and other places in each other's territory as may be agreed to.

Consuls-General, Consuls, vice-consuls and consular agents shall be provided with executors or other valid authorization of their appointment. Such executor or authorization is liable to be withdrawn by the country which issued it, if considered necessary. The reasons for the withdrawal shall be indicated wherever possible.

The persons mentioned above shall enjoy, on a reciprocal basis, all the rights, privileges, exemptions and immunities that are accorded to persons of corresponding status of any other State.

Article 5

The Government of Nepal shall be free to import, from or through the territory of India, arms, ammunition or warlike material and equipment necessary for the security of Nepal. The procedure for giving effect to this arrangement shall be worked out by the two Governments acting in consultation.

Article 6

Each Government undertakes, in token of the neighbourly friendship between India and Nepal, to give to the nationals of the other, in its territory, national treatment with regard to participation in industrial and economic development of such territory and to the grant of concessions and contracts relating to such development.

Article 7

The Governments of India and Nepal agree to grant, on a reciprocal basis, to the nationals of one country in the territories of the other the same privileges in the matter of residence, ownership of property, participation in trade and commerce, movement that privileges of a similar nature.

Article 8

So far as matters dealt with herein are concerned, this Treaty cancels all previous treaties, agreements, and engagements entered into on behalf of India between the British Government and the Government of Nepal.

Article 9

This Treaty shall come into force from the date of signature by both Governments.

Article 10

The Treaty shall remain in force until it is terminated by either party by giving one year's notice.

Done in duplicate at Kathmandu this 31st day of July, 1950.

(Sd.)

Chandreshwar Prasad Narain Singh

For the Government of India

(Sd.)

Mohan Shamsher Jang Bahadur Rana

For the Government of Nepal

Annexure 2

Letter from the Ambassador of India to the Prime Minister of Nepal Kathmandu, 31st July 1950

Your Highness,

In the course of our discussion of the Treaties of Peace and Friendship and of Trade and Commerce which have been happily concluded between the Government of India and the Government of Nepal, we agreed that certain matters of details be regulated by an exchange of letters. In pursuance of this understanding, it is hereby agreed between the two Governments:

Neither Government shall tolerate any threat to the security of the other by a foreign aggressor. To deal with any such threat, the two Governments shall consult with each other and devise effective countermeasures.

Any arms, ammunition or warlike material and equipment necessary for the security of Nepal that the Government of Nepal may import through the territory of India shall be so imported with the assistance and agreement of the Government of India. The Government of India will take steps for the smooth and expeditious transport of such arms and ammunition through India.

In regard to Article 6 of the Treaty of Peace and Friendship which provides for national treatment, the Government of India recognizes that it may be necessary for some time to come to afford the Nepalese nationals in Nepal protection from unrestricted competition. The nature and extent of this protection will be determined as and when required by mutual agreement between the two Governments.

If the Government of Nepal should decide to seek foreign assistance in regard to the development of the natural resources of, or of any industrial project in Nepal, the Government of Nepal shall give first preference to the Government or the nationals of India, as the case may be, provided that the terms offered by the Government of India or Indian nationals, as the case may be, are not less favourable to Nepal than the terms offered by any other foreign Government or by other foreign nationals.

Nothing in the foregoing provision shall apply to assistance that the Government of Nepal may seek from the United Nations Organization or any of its specialized agencies.

Both Governments agree not to employ any foreigners whose activity may be prejudicial to the security of the other. Either Government may make representations to the other in this behalf, as and when occasion requires.

Please accept Your Highness, the assurances of my highest consideration.

(Sd.)

Mohan Shamsher Jang Bahadur Rana

Maharaja, Prime Minister and Supreme Commander-in-Chief of Nepal

Annexure 3

40-Point Demand of the Maoists Submitted to the Government in 1996

4 February, 1996

Right Honourable Prime Minister

Prime Minister's Office,

Singha Darbar, Kathmandu

Sub: Memorandum

Sir,

It has been six years since the autocratic monarchical partyless Panchayat system was ended by the 1990 People's Movement and a constitutional monarchical multiparty parliamentary system established. During this period state control has been exercised by a tripartite interim government, a single-party government of the Nepali Congress, a minority government of UML and a present Nepali Congress-RPP-Sadbhavana coalition. That, instead of making progress, the situation of the country and the people is going downhill is evident from the fact that Nepal has slid to being the second poorest country in the world; people living below the absolute poverty line has gone up to 71 per cent; the number of unemployed has reached more than 10 per cent while the number of people, who are semi-employed or in disguised employment, has crossed 60 per cent; the country is on the verge of bankruptcy due to rising foreign loans and deficit trade; economic and cultural encroachment within the country by foreign, and especially Indian, expansionists is increasing by the day; the gap between the rich and the poor and between towns and villages is growing wider. On the other hand, parliamentary parties that have formed the government by various means have shown that they are more interested in remaining in power with the blessings of foreign imperialist and expansionist masters than in the welfare of the country and the people. This is clear from their blindly adopting so-called privatisation and liberalisation to fulfil the interests of all imperialists and from the recent 'national consensus' reached in handing over the rights over Nepal's water resources to Indian expansionists. Since 6 April, 1992, the United People's Front has been involved in various struggles to fulfil relevant demands related to nationalism, democracy and livelihood, either by itself or with others. But rather than fulfil those demands, the governments formed at different times have violently suppressed the agitators and taken the lives of hundreds; the most recent example of this is the armed police operation in Rolpa a few months back. In this context, we would like to once again present to the current coalition government demands related to nationalism, democracy and livelihood, which have been raised in the past and many of which have become relevant in the present context.

Our Demands

Concerning Nationality

1. All discriminatory treaties, including the 1950 Nepal-India Treaty, should be abrogated.
2. The so-called Integrated Mahakali Treaty concluded on 29 January, 1996 should be repealed immediately, as it is designed to conceal the disastrous Tanakpur Treaty and allows Indian imperialist monopoly over Nepal's water resources.
3. The open border between Nepal and India should be regulated, controlled and systematised. All vehicles with Indian licence plates should be banned from Nepal.
4. The Gurkha/Gorkha Recruitment Centres should be closed. Nepali citizens should be provided dignified employment in the country.
5. Nepali workers should be given priority in different sectors. A 'work permit' system should be strictly implemented if foreign workers are required in the country.

6. The domination of foreign capital in Nepali industries, business and finance should be stopped.
7. An appropriate customs policy should be devised and implemented so that economic development helps the nation become self-reliant.
8. The invasion of imperialist and colonial culture should be banned. Vulgar Hindi films, videos and magazines should be immediately outlawed.
9. The invasion of colonial and imperial elements in the name of NGOs and INGOs should be stopped.

Concerning People's Democracy

10. A new constitution should be drafted by representatives elected for the establishment of a people's democratic system.
11. All special privileges of the king and the royal family should be abolished.
12. The army, the police and the bureaucracy should be completely under people's control.
13. All repressive acts, including the Security Act, should be repealed.
14. Everyone arrested extra-judicially for political reasons or revenge in Rukum, Rolpa, Jajarkot, Gorkha, Kabhrc, Sindhupalchowk, Sindhuli, Dhanusa, Ramechhap, and so on, should be immediately released. All false cases should be immediately withdrawn.
15. The operation of armed police, repression and state-sponsored terror should be immediately stopped.
16. The whereabouts of citizens, who disappeared in police custody at different times, namely Dilip Chaudhary, Bhuwan Thapa Magar, Prabhakar Subedi and others, should be investigated and those responsible brought to justice. The families of victims should be duly compensated.
17. All those killed during the People's Movement should be

declared martyrs. The families of the martyrs and those injured and deformed should be duly compensated, and the murderers brought to justice.

18. Nepal should be declared a secular nation.
19. Patriarchal exploitation and discrimination against women should be stopped. Daughters should be allowed access to paternal property.
20. All racial exploitation and suppression should be stopped. Where ethnic communities are in the majority, they should be allowed to form their own autonomous governments.
21. Discrimination against downtrodden and backward people should be stopped. The system of untouchability should be eliminated.
22. All languages and dialects should be given equal opportunities to prosper. The right to education in the mother tongue up to higher levels should be guaranteed.
23. The right to expression and freedom of press and publication should be guaranteed. The government mass media should be completely autonomous.
24. Academic and professional freedom of scholars, writers, artists and cultural workers should be guaranteed.
25. Regional discrimination between the hills and the tarai should be eliminated. Backward areas should be given regional autonomy. Rural and urban areas should be treated at par.
26. Local bodies should be empowered and appropriately equipped.

Concerning Livelihood

27. Land should belong to 'tenants'. Land under the control of the feudal system should be confiscated and distributed to the landless and the homeless.
28. The property of middlemen and comprador capitalists

should be confiscated and nationalized. Capital lying unproductive should be invested to promote industrialization.

29. Employment should be guaranteed for all. Until such time as employment can be arranged, an unemployment allowance should be provided.
30. A minimum wage for workers in industries, agriculture and so on should be fixed and strictly implemented.
31. The homeless should be rehabilitated. No one should be relocated until alternative infrastructure is guaranteed.
32. Poor farmers should be exempt from loan repayments. Loans taken by small farmers from the Agricultural Development Bank should be written off. Appropriate provisions should be made to provide loans for small farmers.
33. Fertilizer and seeds should be easily available and at a cheap rate. Farmers should be provided with appropriate prices and markets for their produce.
34. People in flood and drought-affected areas should be provided with appropriate relief materials.
35. Free and scientific health services and education should be available to all. The commercialization of education should be stopped.
36. Inflation should be checked. Wages should be increased in proportionate to inflation. Essential goods should be cheaply and easily available to everyone.
37. Drinking water, roads and electricity should be provided to all villagers.
38. Domestic and cottage industries should be protected and promoted.
39. Corruption, smuggling, black marketing, bribery, and the practices of middlemen and so on should be eliminated.
40. Orphans, the disabled, the elderly and children should be duly honoured and protected.

We would like to request the present coalition government to immediately initiate steps to fulfil these demands, which are inextricably linked with the Nepali nation and the life of the people. If there are no positive indications towards this from the government by 17 February, 1996, we would like to inform you that we will be forced to adopt the path of armed struggle against the existing state power.

Thank you.

Dr. Baburam Bhattarai

Chairman

Central Committee, United People's Front, Nepal

Annexure 4

Nepal Prime Minister Sher Bahadur Deuba's Address to the Nation after Declaring the State of Emergency, November 28, 2001

In the aftermath of the wave of attacks carried out by Maoist insurgents across Nepal on November 23, 2001, the government imposed a State of Emergency on November 26. Two days later, the then Prime Minister addressed the nation outlining the reasons for the imposition of emergency and the government's response to the Maoist attacks. The full text of the address is reproduced.

Today our country is passing through a difficult situation. Terrorists by the name of Maoists have terrorized Nepalese life through killings, violence and bloodshed. Despite this, we invited them to the negotiating table for a peaceful resolution to our differences and country's problems so as to give an outlet to the problem. In fact the talks with the Maoists and the efforts for peaceful solution were not only the desire of the government, but also of the entire nation.

However, the Maoist group has taken to the path of causing serious setbacks to the fabric of national unity and security by means of violence, terrorism and killings. We showed utmost flexibility to bring the Maoist group that was expanding its activities through violence for the past six years into the mainstream of politics. But the Maoist terrorists totally ignored our honest efforts and people's wishes. At a time when our view that counter-violence cannot be an answer to violence has suffered a setback, the government has arrived at a decision of mobilizing all its security agencies to control such activities.

We patiently discussed their demands and requests with a hope that we could bring them into the mainstream of Nepali politics and society through talks based on mutual trust. And we made efforts to give space to the possibilities of peace and building of a violence free civilized society. In course of facilitating and building a more congenial atmosphere for talks, we even fulfilled their many demands. Though they treated the Nepalese people and democracy as enemies, the government as a propagator of democratic culture did not behave with them as an enemy. Efforts were made to bring those who had lost their ways onto the right path.

Even after an understanding was reached to enter into talks by halting violence and murder and even after the talks got off the ground, the Maoists continued to engage in different criminal activities. They looted food grains from farmers and indulged in violence. They made assaults on religious ceremonies and faiths of people. They kept on attacking the institution of monarchy—the symbol of faith of Nepali people, the constitution, multi-party democracy and basic human rights. They made attempts to disturb social goodwill and weaken national unity and integrity.

We were optimistic of the possibility of hammering out a peaceful solution. But the group called the Maoists perpetrated violence and bloodbath unparalleled in the history of peaceful Nepal. The country was optimistic of arriving at a certain conclusion through peace talks. Three rounds of talks were already held and we were in preparation for the fourth round of talks. But the Maoists unilaterally broke the dialogues and peace efforts all of a sudden. Consequently, the nation once again has bogged down in a vicious cycle of violence, killings and terrorism.

In utter disregard to the government's efforts and people's goodwill, the Maoist terrorists carried out attacks on the innocent people, political party workers, civil servants, etc. They even attempted to hurt the national integrity by assaulting the security personnel including police and army.

His Majesty's Government has decided to declare a State of Emergency in the country to prevent the worse situation in the country from being further deteriorated. Maintenance of peace and order by mobilizing security agencies has become our foremost duty and necessity. Though the declaration will cause some discomfort to the people, the inconvenience caused by the declaration is minimal as compared to the one caused by terrorism widespread in the nation.

I am fully convinced that all Nepali people, political parties and the civic society is aware of the fact that a government accountable to the people won't take such a difficult decision if there was affordable situation in the country.

I am also fully convinced that all political parties and every section of the civic society will extend their cooperation to the government in the present difficult situation. The government will be fully alert on civic liberty even if emergency has been declared. Necessary legal provisions will be made so that the civic society is least affected. But there may be still some inconvenience during emergency. In the present situation, all Nepali people should be united for the sake of public interest, monarchy, the present constitution, multi-party democracy and the welfare of Nepal and remain committed to root out terrorism.

I am of the belief that the attention of the nation and the people will be focused on peace and order rather than on discomfort, which is only for short time. At this time of great challenge, which the country is passing through, the government is with the people because it is not a separate entity aloof from the people. It is the foremost duty of the government to provide security to the life and property of the people.

I make an earnest appeal to all Nepalese brothers and sisters to focus our power and attention against terrorism so that we can shoulder the serious responsibility successfully. Encouraging terrorism under any pretext will be considered as a serious crime against the country, people and democracy.

All the persons, groups and institutions within and outside the country aiding and abetting terrorism through a supply of arms, money and information have to be brought under the purview of law and punished accordingly. I expect cooperation and guidance from all political parties, entire mass media and civic society in this national campaign.

His Majesty's Government will bring the terrorists before the people and to book. I want to assure the nation and the people that the security agencies of the government are capable of materializing people's desires and resolve of putting the violence and terror to an end for good.

The government will move ahead by reaching an understanding with all political parties for social and economic reforms and development and for consolidating security arrangements. The cooperation of the civic society and the political parties in this endeavour is most crucial. I want to state here that all friendly countries and institutions having goodwill towards Nepal democracy in the country are with the Nepalese people and His Majesty's Government in combating terrorism.

Annexure 5

Proclamation to the Nation by King Gyanendra on February 1, 2005

On February 1, 2005, King Gyanendra dismissed the Government headed by Prime Minister Sher Bahadur Deuba and imposed a state of Emergency in Nepal. Following is the full text of his proclamation:

Beloved Countrymen,

1. The Kingdom of Nepal was built on the foundations of the unification process initiated by King Prithvi Narayan Shah the Great. It is well known that to reign in accordance with the people's aspirations, our forefathers initiated revolutionary measures of historic importance, ensuring a bright future of the nation and her people. History is witness to the fact that both the Nepalese people and the King have, in unison, played decisive roles in each and every period of the Kingdom's process of unification, democratisation and modernisation.

2. Today, we have once again reached a juncture where, in keeping with popular aspirations, a historic decision must be taken to defend multiparty democracy by restoring peace for the nation and people. Even when bloodshed, violence and devastation has pushed the country on the brink of destruction, those engaged in politics in the name of the country and people continue to shut their eyes to their welfare. Tussle for power, abuse of authority on gaining power and unhealthy competition in fulfilling personal and communal interests at the expense of the nation and citizenry contributed to further deterioration in the situation. There were attempts to flout the universally accepted rule of law in the name of politics. Our desire to ensure social, political and economic justice for our beloved people through the meaningful exercise of multiparty democracy could not be materialised. There was a steady rise in crimes against the nation and people, including destruction of development infrastructures

constructed for the people's benefit. Whereas all democratic forces should have adopted a unified approach against terrorism, leaders instead continued their tussle for power, encouraging simple political workers to vandalise public utilities in the name of politics. Faced with this steadily declining situation, it is now time to bring to an end the ongoing acts of terrorist violence and pledge, in earnest, to fulfil the people's aspirations with the restoration of peace and security in the country.

Beloved Countrymen,

3. Democracy and progress always complement each other. But, Nepal's bitter experiences over the past few years tend to show that democracy and progress contradict one another. Multiparty democracy was discredited by focusing solely on power politics. Parliament witnessed many aberrations in the name of retaining and ousting governments. Not a single House of Representatives was allowed to complete its tenure. Continuous confusion and disorder resulted in the obstruction of the democratic process. While the people's aspirations continued to be shattered and their trust trampled on, they became increasingly disenchanted with democracy itself. After being incapable of holding elections, there were conspiracies to form undemocratic governments, which would be responsible to no one. There was also a written consensus amongst all political parties on vacuuming the people's representatives out but they could not see eye to eye when it came to working together in filling this void. The participation and concurrence of political parties in making way for a form of governance, which negated popular representation, was against the people's wishes and norms and spirit of multiparty democracy. So, we appealed to all those who have faith in democracy with the intention of activating, at the earliest, the system of popular representation. We also met a number of times with members of the general public, senior citizens, representatives of the civil society and leaders of political parties in our effort to gauze the popular mandate and try to convince them of the country's requirements and people's aspirations. We reminded them that the only wish of the Nepalese

people and friends of Nepal was to bring to an end the ongoing violence and destructive activities and return peace and tranquillity to the country without any further delay. In order to conduct the general elections in an environment of peace and security, opportunities were given to leaders of various political parties to constitute the Council of Ministers, with executive power. But the situation did not improve. National politics was plagued by not uniting in running the government, but opposing it on being ousted from it. No serious efforts were made to attenuate the real threat posed against democracy by terrorism in the form of a single-party autocracy. The habit of passing carefree remarks on matters of national security continued. Political parties were unable to display responsible behaviour in augmenting the patriotic fervour of our dutiful security personnel, who are active round the clock in ensuring security of the nation and people. Multiparty democrats could not sincerely unite, with national interest as the focal point, to forever end the cycle of devastation being lashed out against the nation and people. Likewise, political parties also could not identify national priorities in keeping with the people's aspirations.

4. Throughout history, the Nepalese people never had to bear the burden of such terrorism, agony and exploitation. No democracy has ever had to go through such a dismal situation, where the innocents are punished by criminals, people whose property is seized and innocent children, women and the elderly, who are mercilessly killed by criminals, cannot receive any kind of protection from those, who govern in their name and parties, who claim to represent the people, do not act in their defence. The nefarious designs of an individual or group, negating the wishes of the Nepalese people as well as the national interest and acting through sponsored mobs, cannot form our national agenda. Conscientiousness towards our responsibility to the future of the country and people has nudged us many a time. Circumstances have reached such a critical stage that it has now become imperative for us to take a decision in the greater interest of the nation and people in accordance with their aspirations.

Beloved Countrymen,

5. Nepal's independence, national unity and sovereignty are best safeguarded by the intimate relationship between the King and the people. An Institution of Monarchy ever devoted to the country and people and people with an innate love for their land is the glorious history of the Kingdom of Nepal, its present and also its future. In keeping with this glorious tradition, popular will as always remained the guiding light for Nepal's Monarchy. We are committed to social justice; totalitarianism and authoritarianism are entirely inconsistent with the Monarchical traditions of the Shah Dynasty. We are convinced of the fact that the Nepalese people have deep faith in and are firmly committed to Constitutional Monarchy and multiparty democracy. We believe that the centralisation of authority is against democratic norms. We feel that a meaningful exercise in democracy can take place only when elected representatives at all levels are given their share in the governance of the country in accordance with the principles of separation of powers. It is our desire that, while no Nepalese should experience pain or suffering, every citizen should have unfettered access to social, economic and political justice. We strongly believe that the people should always feel that their wishes are being fully honoured and their interests completely protected in the governance of the country. It is our desire to ensure that the Kingdom of Nepal forges ahead towards the creation of a mature democracy and welfare society with the collective judgment, understanding and farsightedness of all patriotic democrats. We are confident that there can never be any differences among democrats on achieving the fundamental objectives of national welfare.

6. We have no interest other than the restoration of sustainable peace and exercise in meaningful democracy for the welfare of Nepal and Nepalese people. Monarchy is guided not by cheap popularity, but by the overall welfare and continued progress of Nepal and her people. Everyone should respect the people's desire for effective reforms. Let no Nepalese feel compelled to take up arms as a means of expressing frustration or disenchantment. At the same time, it must be ensured that every citizen has the opportunity to express discontent effectively without jeopardizing social harmony. It is clear

that what the people want are a meaningful exercise in democracy, an effective market economy, good governance, transparency and a corruption-free rule of law. Our only wish is to guarantee our people's happiness through democracy, instil hope among the youth for a brighter future and to ensure dignity for Nepal amongst the comity of nations. Equal opportunities for the development of all our languages, peoples and their cultures alone can preserve and consolidate the Kingdom's distinct characteristics.

7. Contrary to the wishes of the Nepalese people, on whom sovereignty is vested, no serious efforts were made towards initiating elections to the House of Representatives within the year 2061 B.S. by maintaining, to the extent possible, peace and security. Instead of preparing the electorate and political parties for the elections and laying the necessary legal, managerial and technical groundwork, time was wasted on paying only lip service on the urgency of holding elections. As it is our responsibility to preserve our nationalism, national unity and sovereignty, as well as to maintain peace and security in the country and ensure that the state of the nation does not deteriorate any further, we have, by virtue of the State Authority as exercised by us and in keeping with the spirit of the Constitution of the Kingdom of Nepal — 1990, taking into consideration Article 27 (3) of the Constitution, dissolved, effective from today, the current Council of Ministers to fulfil the people's desire for the restoration of peace and security and to activate soon the democratic dispensation. The Council of Ministers to be constituted will be under our Chairmanship. This Council of Ministers will give utmost priority to reactivating multiparty democracy in the country within three years with the implementation of effective reforms by restoring peace and security.

Beloved Countrymen,

8. Only a meaningful multiparty democracy can be an effective means of governance by the people. A successful multiparty democracy alone is synonymous with people's democracy. Such a system, which is people-oriented, mature, cultured and refined, has been disrupted.

Terrorising the innocent population, extorting money through intimidation, brutally murdering those who dissent, kidnapping students and perpetrating atrocities against teachers, making false promises to simple people and destroying development projects aimed at the people's welfare are crimes against the nation and people, which have to be brought to an immediate end. From now on, such crimes will be dealt with firmly in accordance with the law. Our security forces have been mobilised to carry out their responsibilities more effectively to end terrorism and restore peace and security in the interest of the nation and people. All the organs of the state must remain alert in honouring and upholding human rights. However, it will be unfair to put the state and terrorists on equal footing. We are confident that all peace-loving Nepalese, who have faith in democracy, will, as always, continue to cooperate with the security forces in maintaining peace and tranquillity.

9. We call upon all those who have gone astray, taking up arms against the nation and people, and those who are engaged in criminal activities against peace and democracy to return to the mainstream of national politics peacefully. Ensuring opportunities to freely express one's views with patriotism as the focal point, fulfilling one's aspirations and contributing to the welfare of the nation and people are the inherent features of multiparty democracy. We assure all those who avail of this opportunity to join the national mainstream that the state will give them opportunities and rights equal to those enjoyed by all our citizens, without any discrimination whatsoever; neither the people nor the law will tolerate any terrorist activities against the state or its citizens.

Beloved Countrymen,

10. We would like to thank all the friendly nations, who have generously supported us, appreciating our commitment to fight terrorism, as well as donors and international financial institutions that have rendered invaluable assistance in our development endeavours. Even the world's democracies are presently faced with the threat of terrorism, which cannot be confined within geographical

boundaries. The world community has in fact realised that the more secure, stable and prosperous the smaller nations become, the more secure, stable and prosperous will the region and the world as a whole be. Nepal is, therefore, committed to eliminating terrorism in her own interest as well as in the interest of democracies around the world. Nepal aspires for peace — for herself, her neighbours and South Asia — and to rid the world of the threat to peace.

11. While expressing our unflinching faith in multiparty democracy, we would like to mention that economic and institutional reforms will continue. Efforts at reforms in the utilisation of public expenditure and public service delivery will be made more effective. Banking discipline will be restored. Measures will be adopted towards the effective implementation of the poverty reduction strategy and the anti-corruption drive. Sustainable development is now our national agenda. No one will be allowed to jeopardise the people's security and the future of democracy. Nepal will not allow terrorists to use her territory against herself or against any other friendly nation. In our ties with other countries, emphasis will be laid on fostering constructive relations based on mutual benefit and pragmatism.

12. Corruption, which has been continuously spreading its tentacles, has not only cast a shadow over politics and administration, but has also obstructed the nation's march towards progress. Corruption has struck at the very core of our society, as a result of which the common man's confidence in the laws of the land has been shaken. Therefore, in keeping with the popular will and to fulfil the main criterion of good governance, effective measures will be adopted to curb corruption, while ensuring that the principles of justice are not infringed upon.

13. It is our desire that democracy be a way of life, politics be conducted in keeping with democratic norms and values, people from all strata of society honestly adhere to democratic ideals and everyone be guided by the interest of the country and people. All Nepalese wish to see our country as a progressive nation, occupying a pride of place in the international community, where democratic ideals thrive in a peaceful environment. It is our belief that upholding human rights not only preserves and promotes democratic values, but also

enhances a way of life and civilisational values commensurate with the 21st century.

Beloved Countrymen,

14. Our decision should leave no room for confusion amongst the security personnel and civil servants in discharge of their duties and responsibilities. Today, it is we Nepalese, who must take an initiative to ensure a bright future for Nepal and the Nepalese. An independent press serves as the medium for raising the level of democratic consciousness. It plays a crucial role in the promotion of national interests. We believe that the press will make effective contributions in ensuring that democratic norms and values inspire our way of life as well as governance. We are confident that, with this in mind, all those, who have faith in multiparty democracy, will discharge their duties from their respective places and the people's aspirations along with the country's requirements will be realised through the shared efforts of all the countrymen.

15. Today, the nation has made a firm commitment and a decision has also been taken accordingly. The nation has taken a step forward towards democracy and progress, leaving behind violence, insecurity and conflict. At a time when the country is in the grip of terrorism, all those who believe in democracy and peace must unite. Let us, therefore, be inspired by our collective wisdom and guided by our national perspective. Any nefarious attempts at disturbing peace and security and hindering efforts at making democracy meaningful will not be tolerated either by the nation or people. Yet, in pursuit of liberalism, we should never overlook an important aspect of our conduct, namely discipline. This is also the thinking of the 21st century. We wish to repeat once again that those, who cannot do justice to Nepal, those who cannot believe in the sound judgment of the people and those who cannot stand in favour of peace, will stand condemned by the motherland.

May Lord Pashupatinath bless us all!

Jaya Nepal!

Annexure 6

12-Point Understanding between seven political parties and the Communist Party of Nepal (Maoist) on November 22, 2005

The long struggle between absolute monarchy and democracy in Nepal has now reached a very grave and new turn. Establishing peace by resolving the 10-year old armed conflict through a forward-looking political outlet has become the need of today. Therefore, implementing the concept of absolute democracy through a forward-looking restructuring of the state has become an inevitable need to solve the problems related to class, caste, gender, region, etc. of all sectors including political, economic, social and cultural, bringing autocratic monarchy to an end and establishing absolute democracy. We make public that, against this existing backdrop and reference in the country, the following understanding has been reached between the seven parliamentary parties and the CPN (Maoist) through different methods of talks.

Points of Understanding

1. Today, democracy, peace, prosperity, social advancement and a free and sovereign Nepal is the chief wish of all Nepalese. We completely agree that autocratic monarchy is the main hurdle in (realising) this. It is our clear view that without establishing absolute democracy by ending autocratic monarchy, there is no possibility of peace, progress and prosperity in the country. Therefore, an understanding has been reached to establish absolute democracy by ending autocratic monarchy, with all forces against the autocratic monarchy centralizing their assault against autocratic monarchy from their respective positions, thereby creating a nationwide storm of democratic protests.

2. The seven agitating parties are fully committed to the fact that only by establishing absolute democracy through the restoration of the Parliament with the force of agitation, forming an all-party government with complete authority, holding elections to a constituent assembly through dialogue and understanding with the Maoists, can the existing conflict in the country be resolved and sovereignty and state power completely transferred to the people. It is the view and commitment of the CPN (Maoist) that the above mentioned goal can be achieved by holding a national political conference of the agitating democratic forces, and through its decision, forming an interim government to hold constituent assembly elections. An understanding has been reached between the agitating seven parties and the CPN (Maoist) to continue dialogue on this procedural work-list and find a common understanding. It has been agreed that the force of people's movement is the only alternative to achieve this.
3. Today, the country has demanded the establishment of permanent peace along with a positive solution to the armed conflict. Therefore, we are committed to ending autocratic monarchy and the existing armed conflict, and establishing permanent peace in the country through constituent assembly elections and forward-looking political outlet. The CPN (Maoist) expresses its commitment to move along the new peaceful political stream through this process. In this very context, an understanding has been reached to keep, during the holding of constituent assembly elections after ending autocratic monarchy, the armed Maoist force and the royal army under the supervision of the United Nations or any other reliable international supervision, to conclude the elections in a free and fair manner and accept the result of the elections. We expect reliable international mediation even during the dialogue process.
4. Expressing clearly and making public institutional commitment to the democratic norms and values like the

competitive multiparty system of governance, civil liberties, human rights, the concept of the rule of law, fundamental rights, etc., the CPN (Maoist) has expressed commitment to move forward its activities accordingly.

5. The CPN (Maoist) has expressed its commitment to create an environment allowing the political activists of other democratic parties displaced during the course of the armed conflict to return to their former localities and live there with dignity, return their home, land and property seized in an unjust manner and carry out their activities without let or hindrance.
6. Undertaking self criticism and self evaluation of past mistakes, the CPN (Maoist) has expressed commitment not to repeat such mistakes in future.
7. The seven political parties, undertaking self evaluation, have expressed commitment not to repeat the mistakes of the past, which were committed while in parliament and in government.
8. In the context of moving the peace process forward, commitment has been expressed to fully respect the norms and values of human rights and press freedom and move ahead accordingly.
9. As the announcement of municipal polls pushed forward with the ill-motive of deluding the people and the international community and giving continuity to the autocratic and illegitimate rule of the King, and the talk of elections to Parliament are a crafty ploy, we announce to actively boycott them and call upon the general public to make such elections a failure.
10. The people and their representative political parties are the real guardians of nationality. Therefore, we are firmly committed to protecting the independence, sovereignty, geographical integrity of the country and national unity. Based on the principle of peaceful co-existence, it is our common obligation to maintain friendly relations with all

countries of the world and good-neighbour relationship with neighbouring countries, especially India and China. But we request the patriotic masses to be cautious against the false attempt by the King and (his) loyalists to prolong his autocratic and illegitimate rule and delude the patriotic people by projecting the illusory "Mandale" nationalism and questioning the patriotism of the political parties, and appeal to the international powers and the people to support, in every possible way, the democratic movement against autocratic monarchy in Nepal.

11. We call upon the civil society, professional organizations, various wings of parties, people of all communities and regions, press and intellectuals to actively participate in the peaceful movement launched on the basis of these understandings centred on democracy, peace, prosperity, forward-looking social change and the country's independence, sovereignty and pride.
12. Regarding the inappropriate conducts that took place between the parties in the past, a common commitment has been expressed to investigate any objection raised by any party over such incidents, take action if found guilty, and to make the action public. An understanding has been reached to settle any problem emerging between the parties through peaceful dialogue at the concerned level or at the leadership level.

Annexure 7
King Gyanendra's Speech, February 1, 2006

On February 1, 2006, on the occasion of the completion of one year of his rule, King Gyanendra addressed the nation. Presented below is the full text of his speech:

Beloved Countrymen,

It is now a year since the decision was taken to restore law and order and activate the multiparty democratic polity in the country in keeping with the nation's needs and the people's aspirations. Arresting a situation that was slipping into anarchy and reactivating a stalled democratic process has not been easy. Yet, given the commitment of our patriotic countrymen, all the Nepalese people have experienced the nation grow in confidence and the self-respect of the Nepalese people restored within a short span of one year, with the cloud of pessimism dissipating. We are confident that, remaining alert to the sensitivities of the self-respecting Nepalese people and our glorious ever independent history, we will be able to ensure for the nation peace, stability and prosperity within the next one year through mutual understanding and with patriotism as the focal point. We believe that a road-map to sustainable peace and reenergising a meaningful democracy are two sides of the same coin. We are confident that a road-map of consensus will forever end all possibilities of resurgence of violence and terrorism in our motherland, which will, otherwise, put at risk the universally acclaimed multiparty democracy and hurt the self-respect of Nepal and the Nepalese people. Guided by a national perspective that upholds our political, administrative and civic traditions, we are confident that by April 2007, all popularly elected bodies will be active in ensuring a bright future for the Nepalese people through a dedicated exercise in democracy so as to create a welfare society.

The nefarious designs to portray Nepal as a failed state a year back has now begun to unravel with acts of terrorism being limited to petty crimes. The elected government not only dissolved the popularly elected village, municipal and district bodies, but also at the national level. The process of activating multiparty democracy and Constitutional Monarchy has now begun with the people exercising their franchise to reinstate these bodies for which the elected government had failed to conduct elections in spite of being given repeated opportunities. The people are determined to ensure the success of the municipal elections currently underway. In fact, the freedom to exercise one's vote through adult franchise forms the democratic basis for an honourable national consensus. Democracy flourishes only through the enfranchisement of the people and democrats are never losers when democracy is upheld. Therefore, the first and foremost preconditions for consolidating democracy are to gain the support of the people through the ballot and respect their mandate. In keeping with these universally accepted democratic principles, the process to reinstate all the elected bodies through free and fair elections has been initiated. We are confident of the active participation of all democrats, who have faith in the people's democratic rights. Democratic norm dictates that, while upholding the people's rights, their confidence can be won only through participation in the democratic process.

Beloved Countrymen,

With efforts to initiate a meaningful exercise in democracy in keeping with the accepted norms, measures are also underway to improve public service utilities for the benefit of the people. As the bureaucracy has been freed of political pressures and discipline instilled among them, criminal activities under political patronage are now under control. The ongoing fiscal and administrative reforms will be implemented in a more effective manner. Rule of law alone will ensure good governance. As long as corruption, which has proved to be a parasite to our society, is allowed to spread its tentacles, a system of governance as aspired by the people cannot be ensured. More effective measures will be adopted to realise the commitment to maintain fiscal discipline. The concept of Land Bank will be effectively implemented to make available land to the landless, agricultural tenants and freed bonded labourers. Internal and external investments will be mobilised to accelerate the pace of economic development, increase employment opportunities, improve transport infrastructure and attain self-sufficiency in the energy sector through optimum utilisation of water resources. An effective integrated policy must be adopted to initiate development activities that have direct impact on the people. A conducive environment exists to utilise the opportunities created by information technology in the economic development of the country. Likewise, the role of the service sector is also increasing in importance. In this context, special programmes will be introduced to create opportunities of self-employment within the country for talented youths. Measures will also be adopted to train those youths going abroad for employment so that their skills and abilities are duly recognised.

The Nepalese are well aware of the fact that character without any moral foundation, politics indifferent to national pride and a form of governance bereft of the people's confidence will neither benefit the nation nor the people. They also know that politics will not have the strength to inspire the people and overcome challenges if it is tainted. It is our belief that multiparty democracy cannot be made meaningful in the absence of significant popular participation in governance, effective decentralisation of authority in the village, municipal, district, zonal and regional levels and maximum autonomy to elected local bodies in the formulation and implementation of development projects.

Democracy can be adopted into our way of life only if we are prepared to have faith in the people's abilities and the elected representatives. To achieve this, guidelines will be formulated in a transparent manner through collective wisdom and reflections based on experiences and aspirations. Appropriate measures will also be initiated to convincingly address, in the greater good of the nation, grievances regarding indigenous people as well as discrimination relating to regional and other issues. Contributing to efforts aimed at the general welfare of the people alone can ensure the collective well-being of the Nepalese. The nation can be freed from the clutches of poverty and made prosperous only through the collective participation of all. We are confident that all Nepalese, conscious of their national pride, will make significant contributions from their respective places towards the success of the pro-development strategies currently being implemented. While history will be the sole judge of an individual or a generation, it should be our endeavour to ensure that the present generation of Nepalese is given due credit.

Beloved Countrymen,

Nepal's foreign policy is now clear and stable. Our foreign policy and relations are solely guided by how best to serve and protect our national interest in a rapidly changing world. This has restored Nepal's prestige and credibility in the international arena. Nepal desires friendship with all and is always ready to cooperate for mutual benefit. Nepal has malice towards none and is ever alert in ensuring that her territory is not used against any friendly country. Nepal is ever ready to have mutually beneficial fruitful relations with both her neighbours. This policy remains unchanged. To act as a catalyst in enhancing economic ties between her two neighbours, Nepal is preparing to be the transit point between them. Nepal's role as a transit point will contribute to the welfare of Nepal, India, China and the region as a whole.

Nepal has unflinching faith in and is totally committed to the principles of human rights. It is in this spirit that our country has adopted the policy of institutionalising the promotion and protection of human rights and rectifying its shortcomings. It is not easy for a country combating terrorism to strike a balance between the compulsions of national security and upholding the rights of the citizens — this is a reality faced by all democratic countries afflicted with the scourge of terrorism. But it is our strong belief that the people must be allowed to exercise their democratic rights in a peaceful manner, with due consideration to national security.

The Nepalese people desire for sustainable peace. This was clearly spelt out to us when we had direct contacts with our beloved people during our recent visits to various parts of the Kingdom. The vigilant Nepalese have well understood the conspiracy to foment further acts of terrorism in the name of momentary cessation of violence. If those, who have gone astray, wish to rejoin the mainstream of peace and creativity, democracy and coordination, and if they wish to dedicate themselves in the service of the people through the ballot, abjuring their murderous acts against the nation and people, we make it clear that they will be given the security and opportunity necessary to shoulder the responsibilities of governance in their capacity as the people's representatives, having won the people's confidence through the universally accepted democratic exercise. The people can be won over only through peaceful political and constructive activities. Activities like disrupting peace, encouraging discord and creating hurdles on the road to rapprochement in the name of democracy will benefit none. Let us, therefore, unite, with patriotism as the focal point, in dedicating ourselves to the people's welfare and initiating a new chapter in the exercise in meaningful democracy. We wish to emphasise that all differences can be resolved within the framework of the Nepalese patriotic tradition in keeping with the Nepalese psyche, which has never had to put up with subjugation throughout history.

Beloved Countrymen,

We have always, single-mindedly and with determination, strived to fulfil our beloved people's aspirations in the greater interest of the motherland. We have no desire other than the Nepalese people's welfare and the responsibility towards Nepal's glorious history. While utilising the indestructible synergy constantly spouting from the fountain head of patriotism, it will be in the interest of the nation to uphold, with utmost dedication, the glorious history of the Kingdom of Nepal. The success of this alone will keep the nation secure and ensure a meaningful democracy for the people.

A clear decision was made for the country last year. Today, let us, once again, pledge to achieve this national goal. The Nepalese are determined to see a peaceful, prosperous and democratic Nepal in tune with the 21st century. The essence of Nepal's glorious history is the fact that the Nepalese people themselves determine Nepal's national agenda in the interest of the country and their own.

Patriotism is the only means of creating a democratic society. We, therefore, call upon all Nepalese to consign mutual recrimination to the bitter past and build a secure and prosperous future for the nation and people, while upholding democratic norms.

May Lord Pashupatinath bless us all!

Jaya Nepal!

Annexure 8

King Gyanendra's Proclamation, April 24, 2006

Beloved Countrymen,

Convinced that the source of State Authority and Sovereignty of the Kingdom of Nepal is inherent in the people of Nepal and cognizant of the spirit of the ongoing people's movement as well as to resolve the on-going violent conflict and other problems facing the country according to the road-map of the agitating Seven Party Alliance, (no mention of Maoists) we, through this Proclamation, reinstate the House of Representatives, which was dissolved on 22 May 2002 on the advice of the then Prime Minister in accordance with the Constitution of the Kingdom of Nepal-1990. We call upon the Seven Party Alliance to bear the responsibility of taking the nation on the path to national unity and prosperity, while ensuring permanent peace and safeguarding multiparty democracy. We also summon the session of the reinstated House of Representatives at the Sansad Bhawan, Singha Durbar at 1 P.M. on Friday, 28 April 2006.

We are confident that this House will contribute to the overall welfare of Nepal and the Nepalese people.

We extend our heartfelt condolences to all those, who have lost their lives in the people's movement and wish the injured speedy recovery. We are confident that the nation will forge ahead towards sustainable peace, progress, full-fledged democracy and national unity.

May Lord Pashupatinath bless us all!

Jaya Nepal!

Annexure 9

25-Points Ceasefire Code of Conduct Signed between the Government of Nepal and CPN (Maoist) on May 25, 2006

Preamble:

Respecting the popular mandate expressed through the historic people's movement for total democracy, progress and peace;

Remaining committed towards the Universal Declaration of Human Rights -1948, and fundamental principles and values of international humanitarian law and human rights;

Remaining committed to fulfil the 12-point agreement between the seven political parties and the Maoists;

Remaining committed towards democratic values including the concept of competitive multiparty democracy, civic liberties, fundamental rights, human rights, press freedom and rule of law;

Guaranteeing the fundamental rights of the Nepali people to participate in the process of constitution making through elections to the Constituent Assembly without any fear, threat and violence;

Placing democracy, peace, prosperity, forward-looking social transformation and freedom, sovereignty and dignity of the nation in the centre; and

In order to transform the ceasefire between the Government of Nepal and the CPN (Maoist) into permanent peace and resolve the problems through negotiations, a code of conduct has been issued as follows as per the wishes of the Nepali people:

Guaranteeing Fearless Civilian Life

1. Not to issue any statement or engage in any activities, which could provoke each other.

2. Both the parties shall not mobilise, display or use their armed forces in a manner that could spread fear and terror amongst the people.
3. Not to attack or destroy each other's military or security installations, not to lay down mines or ambushes, not to recruit new people in one's military and not to spy against each other.
4. Both sides will extend mutual cooperation in order to maintain peace and security.
5. Discussion and understanding will be made as per need regarding the issue of management of arms and armed personnel.

Creating an Environment of Trust among the People

6. Both the parties will not participate in public meetings, conference or any other political activities in combat dresses or along with arms.
7. No hindrance will be made from either side for political activists and members of social organisations to move around the country and express their views, organize meetings or engage in their organisational works. They will not be subject to any mental or physical pressure.

On Basic Services to the People and Development Activities

8. During the period of ceasefire, activities like 'bandh' (general strike) and 'chakka jam' (transport strike) will not be organised, but peaceful demonstrations may be organised.
9. Essential services and facilities to the people will be allowed to operate without any disruption.
10. Not to create hurdles in undertaking regular development works peacefully and other works aimed at people's benefit.
11. Transportation of items like food, medicines, materials used

in development woks and daily utility items will not be obstructed or banned.

12. Both the parties will create an environment for the smooth functioning of schools, colleges and universities, hospitals, health centres and industrial institutions.

Cooperation from Media for Peace Talks

13. Use civilised and dignified language while disseminating information about ceasefire, code of conduct and the peace process and other political activities.
14. Nobody should issue statements through media in a manner, which could hamper the talks and peace process.

    Not to collect donation and other financial assistance forcefully.

15. Donation or financial assistance in cash, kind or in the form of services will not be collected or mobilised against one's will.

Release and Rehabilitation

16. Accusation, claims or cases filed by both the parties against various individuals will be withdrawn and the detainees will be released gradually.
17. Whereabouts of the people, who have been disappeared, will be publicised immediately.
18. To help in the rehabilitation of and extend cooperation to displaced people to return to their respective houses in a peaceful, comfortable and respectable manner.
19. Return the properties of the leaders of political parties, activists and civilians, which were seized, locked up or prohibited from being used during the period of the conflict, to concerned persons or their families. Problems arising while

returning the properties will be resolved through mutual agreement.

Facilitating the Talks

20. No hurdles will be created in the movement and activities of individuals involved in negotiations from both the parties

Monitoring

21. On the basis of mutual agreement between the two parties, national and international monitoring teams will be asked to monitor the ceasefire.

Miscellaneous

22. Dispute, if any, in terms of interpretation of this code of conduct, will be resolved on the basis of agreement between the parties.
23. In accordance with the spirit of the preamble of this code, amendments could be made in the code of conduct through mutual agreement.
24. To enforce this code of conduct immediately after it is signed.
25. To make the code of conduct public immediately after it is signed.

Signed by:
Krishna Bahadur Mahara
On behalf of the CPN (Maoist)

Signed by:
Krishna Prasad Sitaula
On behalf of the Government of Nepal
May 25, 2006

Annexure 10

The Eight-Point SPA-Maoist Agreement Following Summit Talks between the Two Sides at the Prime Minister's Residence at Baluwatar on June 16, 2006

1. Effectively and honestly implement the 12-point understanding reached between the SPA and Maoists in November last year and the 25-point Ceasefire Code of Conduct signed between the SPA government and CPN-Maoist on May 26 this year.
2. Commitment to democratic norms and values including competitive multi-party system, civic liberties, fundamental rights, human rights, press freedom, and the concept of rule of law and carry out each other's activities in a peaceful manner.
3. Request the United Nations to help in the monitoring and management of the armies and arms of both government and Maoist sides for a free and fair election to the Constituent Assembly.
4. Guarantee the democratic rights achieved through the 1990 Popular Movement and the recent historic People's Movement; draft an interim constitution based on the 12-point understanding and the ceasefire Code of Conduct; form an interim government accordingly; announce the dates for constituent assembly elections; dissolve the House of Representatives through consensus after making alternative arrangement; dissolve the People's Governments of CPN-Maoists.
5. Decide issues of national interests having long-term effects through consensus.
6. Guarantee the fundamental right of the Nepali people to

participate in the constituent assembly elections without any fear, influence, threat and violence. Invite international observation and monitoring during the elections as per the need.

7. Bring about a forward-looking restructuring of the state so as to resolve the class-based, racial, regional and gender-based problems through constituent assembly elections. Transform the ceasefire between the Nepal Government and CPN-Maoist into permanent peace by focusing on democracy, peace, prosperity, forward-looking change and the country's independence, sovereignty and pride, and express commitment to resolve the problem through talks.
8. The government and Maoist talks teams have been directed to accomplish all tasks related to above-mentioned points without any delay.

Annexure 11
Six-Point Agreement between SPA and Maoists on November 7, 2006

Respecting people's aspiration for democracy, peace and progress expressed through repeated historic people's movement and struggles since 1951,

Reaffirming commitments to the 12-point and 8-point agreements, and 25-point code of conduct between the seven parties and the Maoists along with other agreements, understandings, code of conducts and letter sent to the United Nations stating similar perspectives by the Maoists and the Nepal government,

Pledging for progressive restructuring of the state by resolving prevailing problems related with class, ethnicity, regional and gender differences,

Reiterating commitments to competitive multiparty democratic system, civil liberties, fundamental rights, human rights, complete press freedom, rule of law and all other norms and values of democratic system,

Guaranteeing the fundamental rights of the Nepalese people to cast their votes in the constituent assembly polls without any kind of fear,

By putting democracy, peace, prosperity, progressive social and economic transformation, independence, integrity, sovereignty and prestige of the state in the centre-stage and to implement the commitments made by both the sides to hold the election to constituent assembly by mid June 2007 in a free and fair manner, the following decisions have been taken from the meeting of the top leaders of the seven parties and the Maoists today, November 8, 2006.

I. Relating to the Implementation of the Past Agreements

Implement all the agreements, understanding and code of conduct signed earlier — fully, sincerely and strongly.

Form a high-level commission to investigate and publicise the whereabouts of citizens stated to have been disappeared by the state and the Maoists in the past.

Accelerate the process of returning the houses, land and properties confiscated in the past. Ensure the environment so that displaced people would be able to return to their villages. For this purpose, committees would be formed in districts comprising representatives from both the sides. Complete all these works within one month.

Make public announcement regarding the withdrawal of all accusations and charges levelled by the state at the leaders and the cadres of the CPN (Maoist) and release all political prisoners from both the sides.

II. Relating to Management of Arms and Army

In order to hold the elections to constituent assembly in a peaceful, free and fair environment and for democratisation and restructuring of the Nepali Army as per the feelings expressed in 12-point agreement, 8-point understanding, 25-point code of conduct and 5-point letter sent to the United Nations, the following works would be carried out:

1. Relating to the Maoist Army

As per the commitments expressed in the letter sent to the United Nations by the Nepal government and the Maoists on August 9, the combatants of the Maoists would be sent to following cantonments. The United Nations would do the necessary verification and monitoring of them.

Main camps would be in the following places:

1. Kailali, 2. Surkhet, 3. Rolpa, 4. Palpa, 5. Kavre, 6. Sindhuli 7. Ilam. There would be three smaller camps located in the periphery of each of these main camps.

All the arms and ammunitions would be securely stored in the camps except those needed for providing security of the camp after the Maoist combatants are sent to the cantonments. They will be put under a single lock system and the concerned side would keep the key of this lock. For the UN to monitor it, a device with siren as well as recording facility will be installed. When there is need to examine the stored arms, the UN would do so in the presence of the concerned side.

Prepare the details of technology including camera for monitoring as per the agreement among the Nepal government, the Maoists and the United Nations.

On completion of cantonment of the Maoist combatants, Nepal government would take up the responsibility for providing ration and other facilities to them.

The interim cabinet would form a special committee to carry out monitoring, integration and rehabilitation of the Maoist combatants.

Make arrangement for the security of the Maoist leaders as per the agreement with the Nepal government

2. Relating to the Nepali Army

The Nepali Army would be confined to the barracks as per the commitments of the letter sent to the United Nations.

Guarantee that its arms would not be used for or against any side.

Keep similar quantity of arms of the Nepali Army in the store, seal it with single-lock system and give the key to the concerned side. For the UN to monitor it, a device with siren as well as recording facility will be installed. When there is need to examine the stored arms, the UN would do so in the presence of the concerned side.

Prepare the details of technology including camera for monitoring as per the agreement among the Nepal government, the Maoists and the United Nations.

The cabinet would control, mobilize and manage the Nepali Army as per the new Military Act. The interim cabinet would prepare and implement the detailed action plan of democratization of the Nepali Army by taking suggestions from the concerned committee of the interim parliament. This includes works like determination of the right number of the Nepali Army, prepare the democratic structure reflecting the national and inclusive character, and train them on democratic principles and human rights values.

Continue the works of the Nepali Army, such as border security, security of the conservation areas, protected areas, banks, airport, power house, telephone tower, central secretariat and security of VIPs.

III. Relating to the Subjects of the Interim Constitution

1. Relating to the Interim Constitution

Finalise the interim constitution presented by the interim constitution drafting committee as per the agreements reached today.

The reinstated House of Representatives would promulgate the interim constitution and the newly formed interim legislature would endorse it.

2. Relating to the Monarchy

No rights on state administration would remain with the King.

Bring the properties of the late King Birendra, late Queen Aishwarya and their family members under the control of the Nepal government and use it for the welfare purposes through a trust.

All properties acquired by King Gyanendra by the virtue of him being the King (like palaces of various places, forests and conservation areas, heritage having historical and archaeological importance) would be nationalised.

Determine the fate of the institution of monarchy by the first meeting of the Constituent Assembly through simple majority vote.

3. Relating to Interim Legislature (Parliament)

The interim legislature would be unicameral of the following type:

- i. There would be 209 members of the seven parties and others, who are members of the present lower and upper house (excluding those, who opposed the people's movement). Since the Left Front does not have its representation in the current parliament, its representation in the interim parliament would be determined based on understanding.
- ii. 73 members from the side of the Maoists.
- iii. 48 members from among the sister organisations and professional bodies, oppressed ethnic communities and regions and political personalities (to be nominated based on understanding) (total number: 330)

But those, who stood against the people's movement, would not be given membership in the interim parliament.

The reinstated House of Representatives and National Assembly would be dissolved once the formation of the interim parliament is complete.

The people's government, people's court run by the CPN (Maoist) would be dissolved on the day of the formation of the interim parliament.

Run the interim parliament as per the political understanding.

4. Relating to interim government

Form the interim cabinet as per the understanding.

Determine the work division and structure of the interim parliament as per understanding.

The interim government would work as per the aspiration of the people's movement, political understanding and culture of cooperation.

5. Relating to Judiciary

Follow the norms and values and concept of the independent judiciary.

Make the judiciary committed to the aspiration of the people's movement, democracy and interim constitution.

Institute a constitutional court to finalise disputes regarding the constituent assembly.

6. Relating to Constitutional Bodies

A new constitutional council will be formed that will include the Prime Minister, Chief Justice and the Speaker of the interim parliament, which will recommend appointments at the constitutional bodies.

Such appointments will be based on specific criteria.

The appointments in the Election Commission will be completed on the basis of understanding.

7. Relating to Local Bodies

Interim local bodies will be formed at district, city and village levels on the basis of agreement between the seven political parties and the Maoists.

8. Relating to Citizenship Problem

Distribute citizenship to all Nepalis, who have been deprived of their citizenship certificate before the election of the constituent assembly.

Considering mid-April 1990 as the base (cut off) year, all Nepalese citizens, who were born before that date and have been continuously living in Nepal since then, will be provided with citizenship certificate.

Other provisions regarding citizenship will be according to the provisions mentioned in the law.

9. Regarding the Election of the Constituent Assembly

The interim cabinet will be given the authority to ascertain the date to hold the election of the constituent assembly by mid-June 2007.

The election of the constituent assembly will be based on mixed electoral system. 205 members will be elected through First-Past-The-Post system. 204 members will be elected as per the proportional representation system on the basis of votes won by the political parties. A law in this regard will be made after consultation with the Election Commission.

While appointing the candidates, the political parties should ensure proportional representation of oppressed groups, regions, *madheshi*, women, *dalit* and other groups. 16 members will be nominated by the interim Council of Ministers from among distinguished persons. The total number of members of the constitutional assembly will be 425.

Nepalese, who are 18 years or above at the time when the interim constitution is promulgated, will be eligible to vote.

Monitoring of the election of the constituent assembly will be done by the United Nations.

10. Structure of the State

To end discriminations based on class, ethnicity, lingual, gender, cultural, religion and region and to deconstruct the centralised and unitary structure of the state and to reconstruct it into an inclusive, democratic and forward looking state.

A high level commission will be formed to suggest on the restructuring of the state.

Final decision regarding the restructuring of the state will be made by the constituent assembly.

11. Directive Principles of Socio-Economic Transformation

To end all forms of feudalism, a common minimum programme will be prepared for socio-economic transformation on the basis of mutual agreement and they will be implemented.

Formulate policies to implement scientific land reform programme by doing away with the feudal land ownership. To adopt policies that will protect and promote national industries and resources.

To ascertain the rights of the citizens on sectors like education, health, shelter, employment and food security.

Policies will be adopted to provide land and socio-economic security to backward groups like landless, bonded labourers, tillers, Haruwa-charuwa and other such groups, which are socio-economically backward.

To adopt policies to take strict actions against the people, who have worked in government positions and have amassed huge amount of properties through corruption.

Prepare a common development concept that will help in socio-economic transformation of the country and will also assist in ensuring the country's prosperity in a short period of time.

Follow policies ascertaining the professional rights of workers and increase investment on sectors like promoting industries, trade and export and increase employment and income generating opportunities.

IV. Relating to the Management of the Conflict Victims

1. Provisions will be made for providing proper relief, respect and resettlement for the family members of the people, who have died due to the conflict and for the ones, who have been disabled.
2. Provide relief to the family members of the people, who have been disappeared on the basis of the report presented by the investigation commission.
3. Carry out special programmes to rehabilitate the people, who have been displaced due to the conflict; to provide relief in case of destruction of private and public properties; and to

reconstruct the destroyed infrastructures.

4. Conduct investigation about those, who were involved in gross violation of human rights at the time of the conflict and those, who committed crime against humanity. Form a high level Truth and Reconciliation Commission to create an environment for social reconciliation.

V. Miscellaneous

1. A high-level committee will be formed as per understanding to monitor if the agreement have been implemented.
2. The government will take action against anyone involved in acting against the code of conduct, agreement and laws.
3. At the time of the election of the constituent assembly, the political parties will be free to present their policies regarding republic, socio-economic transformation, referendum, election system and other such issues in which an agreement has not been reached now.

VI. Time Schedule

1. To conclude comprehensive peace agreement between Nepal government and the CPN (Maoists) by November 16, 2006.
2. That all the Maoist combatants would gather into the camps by November 21, 2006 as stated in 2(1) and store the arms. The United Nations would do their verification and monitoring.
3. As stated in 2(5), the Nepali Army would remain confined in barrack by November 21, 2006; keep the specified number of arms in the store and the United Nations would conduct its monitoring.
4. To complete the interim constitution by November 21, 2006.
5. To promulgate the interim constitution by November 26, 2006; establish the interim legislature and dissolve the House of Representatives and National Assembly.

6. Form the interim cabinet by December 1, 2006.

Prachanda
Chairman, CPN (Maoists)

Girija Prasad Koirala
Prime Minister and President of the Nepali Congress

Madhav Kumar Nepal
General Secretary of CPN (UML)

Sher Bahadur Deuba
President of Nepali Congress Democratic

Amik Sherchan
Deputy Prime Minister and Chairman of People's Front Nepal

Bharat Bimal Yadav
Vice President of NSP (Anandi Devi)

Narayan Man Bijukchhe
President of NWPP

C.P. Mainali
Chairman of Left Front

November 8, 2006

Note of Dissent by the UML

Agreeing for the implementation of the subjects stated above as all other parties have agreement on those, our party has following differences:

1. The UML believes that the issue of whether to keep the monarchy or not should be determined through the referendum along with the election to constituent assembly.
2. The UML believes that it would be most democratic to adopt the proportional system for election to the constituent assembly.

Annexure 12

Comprehensive Peace Accord held between Government of Nepal and CPN (Maoist) on November 21, 2006

Preamble

Respecting popular mandate of Nepali people expressed in favour of democracy, peace and progression through the historical struggles and people's movements, time and again, from 2007 BS and even before till now;

Reaffirming the full commitment towards the twelve-point agreement reached between seven political parties, CPN (Maoist), eight-point consensus, twenty-five point code of conduct held between Government of Nepal and CPN (Maoist), decision made in the meeting held between apex leaders of seven political parties and CPN (Maoist) held on November 8 2006 including all agreement, consensus, code of conduct reached between the Government of Nepal and CPN (Maoist), and letters of similar viewpoints sent to United Nations;

Expressing determination for progressive restructuring of the state to resolve existing problems in the country, based on class, caste, region, sex;

Reiterating the full commitment towards democratic value and acceptance including competitive multiparty democratic system of governance, civil liberty, fundamental rights, human rights, full press freedom and concept of rule of law;

Remaining committed towards Universal Declaration of Human rights, 2048, international humanitarian laws and basic principles and acceptance relating to human rights;

Keeping democracy, peace, prosperity, progressive economic and social change and independence, indivisibility, sovereignty, and self respect of the country at centre;

Expressing commitment to hold election to constituent assembly in free and fair manner till the end of the month of Jeth 2064 BS;

Declaring the beginning of a new chapter of peaceful collaboration by ending armed struggle continued in the country from 2052 BS through political consensus between the two parties to ensure sovereignty of Nepali People through constituent assembly, forward looking political resolution, democratic restructuring of the state and economic-social and cultural transformation;

This comprehensive peace agreement has been reached between the Government of Nepal and CPN (Maoist) with commitment to transform ceasefire between Government of Nepal and CPN (Maoist) into sustainable peace.

1. Preliminary

1.1. The name of this agreement is "Comprehensive Peace Agreement". In short, the agreement shall be called Peace Agreement.

1.2. The agreement shall come into force after public declaration by the government and Maoist side.

1.3. Both the sides shall give necessary directives to all the agencies under their control for immediate implementation of this agreement and to abide by it and implement it and get it implemented.

1.4. All the agreement, consensus and decision reached between seven political parties, the government and Maoists that are enclosed in annex shall be integral part of this agreement.

1.5. The consensus and agreement to be reached hereafter for the implementation of this agreement shall also be integral part of this agreement.

2. Definition

Unless the subject and context mean otherwise, in this agreement:

(a) "Ceasefire" means the acts to negate all forms of aggressions, kidnappings, disappearances, taking into custody aimed at each other and between Government of Nepal and CPN (Maoist), mobilization and strengthening of armed forces, destruction in the society by any means including aggression and activities of violence and acts of incitement and instigation.

(b) "Interim Constitution" means "Interim Constitution of Nepal 2063" to be issued until drafting and enforcement of the new constitution by constituent assembly.

(c) "Interim Council of Ministers" means "Interim Council of Ministers" to be formed according to Interim Constitution.

(d) "Both the Parties" means the party of Government of Nepal and the party of Communist Party of Nepal (Maoist).

(e) "Prevailing Law" means Interim Constitution of Nepal 2063 and prevailing Nepal Laws that are not inconsistent with it. But this definition shall not obstruct legal arrangement existed before enforcement of Interim constitution 2063.

(f) "Verification" means the subject of verification and true record keeping of military, combatant and arms by United Nations.

3. Political-Economic-Social Transformation and Conflict Management

Both the parties are in agreement to adopt following policy and programme for political-economic and social transformation and to affirmatively resolve existing conflict in the country:

3.1. To ensure forward moving political, economic and social transformation on the basis of decision made in summit meeting between seven political parties and CPN (Maoist) held on November 8, 2006 (Annex-6).

3.2. To guarantee sovereignty inherent in Nepalese people in practice by forming interim legislature — parliament according to interim constitution and by holding election to the constituent assembly in free and fair manner till the Month of Jetha, 2064 BS by the Interim Government.

3.3. To not allow any authority regarding affairs of governance of the country to remain with the king. To bring the properties of late King Birendra, late queen Aishwarya and their family under the Government of Nepal and to make use of the property in the interest of the state by forming a trust. To nationalize all the properties (like palaces situated in different places, forest and parks, heritages with historical and archaeological importance) received by King Gyanendra in his capacity as the King. To decide the issue of whether or not to retain the monarchy by simple majority in the first meeting of constituent assembly.

3.4. To adopt a political system that complies with universally accepted fundamental human rights, multiparty competitive democratic system, sovereignty inherited in people, supremacy of the people, constitutional check and balance, rule of law, social justice, equality, independent judiciary, periodic election, monitoring by civil society, complete press freedom, people's right to information, transparency and accountability in the activities of political parties, people's participation, impartial, competent, and fair concept of bureaucracy.

3.5. To address the problems related to women, *dalit*, indigenous people, *janajatis*, *madheshi*, oppressed, neglected, minorities and the backward by ending discrimination based on class, caste, language, sex, culture, religion, and region and to restructure the state on the basis of inclusiveness, democracy and progression by ending present centralized and unitary structure of the state.

3.6. To keep implementing at least programmes of common consensus for the economic and social transformation to end all forms of feudalism.

3.7. To adopt the policy to implement scientific land reform programme by ending feudalistic system of land holding.

3.8. To follow the policy for the protection and promotion of national industries and resources.

3.9. To adopt policy to establish rights of all citizens in education, health, housing, employment and food reserve.

3.10. To adopt policy to provide land and other economic protection to landless squatters, Kamaiya, Halia, Harwa, Charwa and economically backward section.

3.11. To adopt policy to severely punish people amassing properties by means of corruption while remaining in government posts.

3.12. To form common development concept for economic and social transformation and justice and to make the country developed and economically prosperous, at the earliest.

3.13. To follow the policy to increase investment in industries, trade and export promotion in order to increase opportunities for income generation by ensuring professional rights of the labourers.

4. Management of Army and Arms

In order to hold election to constituent assembly in free and fair manner and for the democratic restructuring of the army to proceed with the following works according to twelve point agreement, eight point consensus, twenty-five point code of conduct, five-point letter sent to United Nations and decision taken by summit meeting held on November 8:

Relating to the Maoists' Army

4.1 As per the commitment expressed in the letter sent on behalf of the Government of Nepal and the CPN (Maoist) to the United

Nations on August 9, 2006, the Maoists' Army combatants shall remain within the following Cantonments. The UN shall verify and monitor them.

The main Cantonments shall remain in the following locations:

1. Kailali 2. Surkhet 3. Rolpa 4. Nawalparasi 5. Chitwan 6. Sindhuli 7. Ilam

Three sub-cantonments shall be placed in the periphery of each of these main cantonments.

4.2. After placing the Maoist combatants within the Cantonments, all the arms and ammunition except those required for providing security to the Cantonments shall be securely stored and the keys to the single lock shall remain with the side concerned. The UN shall monitor the process of placing the weapons under the single lock by keeping records and fitting a device along with siren. In case of need to examine the weapons placed under the single lock, the UN shall do so under the presence of concerned side. All the technical details along with Camera Monitoring shall be prepared under the joint agreement of the UN, CPN (Maoist) and the Government of Nepal.

4.3. The Government of Nepal shall make all the necessary arrangements including ration needed for the Maoist combatants after placing them within the Cantonments.

4.4. The Interim Council of Ministers shall form a special committee in order to inspect, integrate and rehabilitate the Maoist combatants.

4.5. The government shall be taking care of security arrangements of the Maoist leaders.

Relating to the Nepali Army

4.6. As per the commitment expressed in the letter sent to the UN, the Nepali Army shall be confined within the barracks. Guarantee that the arms shall not be used for or against any side. The Nepali Army shall store the same amount of arms in accordance with that of the Maoists and seal it with single-lock and give the key to the concerned side. In case of need to examine the stored arms, the UN would do so in the presence of the concerned side. Prepare the details of technology including camera for monitoring as per the agreement among the Government of Nepal, the Maoists and the UN.

4.7. The Council of Ministers shall control, mobilize and manage the Nepali Army as per the new Military Act. The Interim Council of Ministers shall prepare and implement the detailed action plan of democratization of the Nepali Army by taking suggestions from the concerned committee of the Interim Parliament. This shall include tasks, such as determining the right number of the Nepali Army, preparing the democratic structure reflecting the national and inclusive character and training them as per the democratic principles and values of the human rights.

4.8. Nepali Army shall be giving continuity to tasks, such as border security, security of the conservation areas, protected areas, banks, airport, power house, telephone tower, central secretariat and security of VIPs.

5. Cease-Fire

5.1. Termination of military action and armed mobilization:

5.1.1. Both sides shall express commitment to refrain from carrying out following activities:

a. Direct or indirect use of any type of weapon or acts of attack against each other.
b. Searching or confiscating weapons belonging to other side with or without weapons at the place where the arms have been stored as per the understanding reached between both sides.
c. Hurt or render mental pressure against any individual.
d. Set up ambush targeting any side.
e. Involve in murder or violent activities.
f. Involvement in kidnap/detention/imprisonment/disappearance

g. Arial attack or bombardment.
h. Mining and sabotaging.
i. Spying military activities of any side.

5.1.2. Both sides shall not recruit additional armed forces or conduct military activities, including transporting weapons, ammunitions and explosives.

However, the security forces deployed by the interim government shall have authority to conduct routine patrol, explore in order to prevent illegal trafficking of the weapons, explosives or raw materials used in assembling weapons at the international border or custom points and seize it.

5.1.3. No individual or group shall bear any illegal weapons, ammunitions or explosives while travelling.

5.1.4. Both sides shall assist each other to mark the landmines and booby-traps used during the time of armed conflict by providing necessary information within 30 days and defuse and excavate it within 60 days.

5.1.5. Armies of both sides shall not bear arms or show their presence wearing combat fatigue during any public programme, political meeting or civil assembly.

5.1.6. Nepal Police and Armed Police Force shall give continuity to the task of maintaining legal system and law and order along with criminal investigation as per the norms and sentiments of the Jana Andolan and peace accord as well as prevailing law.

5.1.7. Both sides shall issue circular to its respective armed bodies or personnel to stop addressing any armed personnel of opposite side by the term 'enemy' or behave in similar manner.

5.1.8. Both sides agree to maintain a record of the government, public, private building, land and other property seized, locked up or not allowed to use in course of the armed conflict and return them back immediately.

5.2 Situation Normalization Measures:

5.2.1. Collection of cash or kind and tax collection against one's wish and against the existing law shall not be allowed.

5.2.2. Both sides agree to make public the status of the people under one's custody and release them within 15 days.

5.2.3. Both sides also agree to make public within 60 days of signing of the agreement the real name, caste and address of the people made 'disappeared' or killed during the conflict and also inform the family members about it.

5.2.4. Both sides agree to constitute a National Peace and Rehabilitation Commission and carry out works through it to normalize the adverse situation arising as a result of the armed conflict, maintain peace in the society and run relief and rehabilitation works for the people victimized and displaced as a result of the conflict.

5.2.5. Both sides agree to set up a High-level Truth and Reconciliation Commission as per the mutual consensus in order to probe about those involved in serious violation of human rights and crime against humanity in course of the armed conflict and develop an atmosphere for reconciliation in the society.

5.2.6. Both sides pledge to abandon all types of war, attack, counter-attack, violence and counter-violence in the country with a commitment to ensure Loktantra, peace and forward-looking change in the Nepali society. It is also agreed that both the sides would assist one another in the establishment of peace and maintaining of law and order.

5.2.7. Both sides guarantee to withdraw accusations, claims, complaints and under-consideration cases levelled against various individuals due to political reasons and immediately make public the state of those imprisoned and immediately release them.

5.2.8. Both sides express the commitment to allow without any political prejudice the people displaced due to the armed conflict to return back voluntarily to their respective ancestral or former residence, reconstruct the infrastructure destroyed as a result of the conflict and rehabilitate and reintegrate the displaced people into the society.

5.2.9. Both sides agree to take individual and collective responsibility of resolving, with also the support of all political parties, civil society and local institutions, any problems arising in the aforementioned context on the basis of mutual consensus and creating an atmosphere conducive for normalization of mutual relations and for reconciliation.

5.2.10. Both sides express the commitment not to discriminate against or exert any kind of pressure on any member of the family of the two sides or on the basis of being related to one another.

5.2.11. Both sides agree not to create any kind of obstacle and allow any kind of obstruction to be created in independent travelling, assuming of duties and executing of work by the Government of Nepal and Public Bodies' employees and assist them in their work.

5.2.12. Both sides agree to allow unrestricted travelling as per the law within the state of Nepal to the United Nations, International Donor Agencies and Diplomatic Missions based in Nepal, National and International Non-Government Organizations,

Press, Human Rights Activists, Election Observers and foreign tourists.

5.2.13. Both sides are committed to operating publicity programmes in a decent and respectable manner.

6. End of Conflict

6.1. On the basis of the historical agreement reached between the Seven Political Parties and the CPN (Maoist) on November 8, 2006, we declare an end to the armed conflict ongoing in the country since 1995 by giving permanency to the ongoing cease-fire between the Government and the Maoists.

6.2. The decisions taken by the meeting on November 8, 2006 of the senior leaders of the Seven Parties and the CPN (Maoist) would be the main policy basis for long-term peace.

6.3. Following the arrival of the Nepali Army in the barracks and the Maoist Army combatants in temporary camps, holding, display and use of violence and arms for creating fear and terror and in any form against the agreement and law would be legally punishable.

6.4. Army of both the sides would not be allowed to publicize for or against any side and support or protest any side. But they shall not be deprived from their right to vote.

7. Human Rights, Fundamental Rights and Adherence to Humanitarian Law

By remaining committed to the Universal Declaration of Human Rights, 1948, the International Humanitarian Law and fundamental principles and standards of human rights, both sides expressed their agreement to the following issues:

7.1. *Human Rights*:

7.1.1. Both sides reiterate their commitment to the respect and protection of human rights and to international humanitarian law and accept that nobody should be discriminated against on the basis of colour, gender, language, religion, age, race, national and social origin, wealth, disability, birth and other status, thought or belief.

7.1.2. Both sides agree to create an atmosphere where the Nepali people can enjoy their civil, political, economic, social and cultural rights and are committed to ensuring that such rights are not violated under any circumstances in the future.

7.1.3. Both sides express the commitment that impartial investigation and action as per the law would be carried out against the people responsible in creating obstructions to the exercising of the rights envisaged in the letter of agreement and guarantee not to encourage impunity. Apart from this, they shall also guarantee the right to relief of the families of the conflict and torture victims and the disappeared.

7.1.4. Both sides would not be involved in the acts of torture, kidnapping and forcing the civilians in any work and take necessary action to discourage such acts.

7.1.5. On the basis of norms and values of secularism, both sides shall respect the social, cultural, religious sensitivity, religious site and the religious faith of the individual.

7.2. *Right to Live:*

7.2.1. Both sides respect and protect the fundamental right to live of an individual. Nobody shall be deprived of this fundamental right and no law shall be formulated to award death penalty.

7.3. *Right to Individual Dignity, Freedom and Mobility*

7.3.1. Both sides respect and protect the right to individual dignity. In this connection, no person including those deprived of enjoying freedom as per the law would be subjected to torture or any other cruel, inhuman or degrading behaviour or punishment. The citizen's right to confidentiality shall be respected.

7.3.2. Both sides shall fully respect the individual's right to freedom and security and shall not be allowed to keep anyone under arbitrary or illegal detention, kidnap or hold captive. Both sides agree to make public the status of every individual made 'disappeared' and held captive and inform about this to their family members, legal advisor and other authorized person.

7.3.3. Both sides shall respect and protect the citizens' right to free mobility and the freedom to choose within legal norms the location of one's residence and express the commitment to respect the right of the people displaced by the conflict and their families to return back to their homes or to settle in any other location of their choice.

7.4. *Civil and Political Rights:*

7.4.1. Both sides are committed to respect the individual's freedom of speech, expression, setting up organizations and holding peaceful gatherings and right to freedom of exploitation.

7.4.2. Both sides respect the right of every citizen to take part directly or through one's selected representative in issues of public concern, to vote, to be elected and equality in joining of public services.

7.4.3. Both sides are committed to respect the individual's right to be informed.

7.5. *Economic and Social Rights:*

7.5.1. Both sides are committed to respect and protect the individual's right to livelihood through employment of their choice or acceptance.

7.5.2. Both sides are committed to respecting and guaranteeing the rights of food security of all the people. They guarantee that there would be no interference in the transportation, use and distribution of food, food products and food grains.

7.5.3. Both sides identify with the fact that the citizens' right to health should be respected and protected. Both sides will not create hurdles in the supply of medicines and in health assistance and campaigns, and express commitment for treatment and rehabilitation of the people injured in course of the conflict.

7.5.4. With the realization of the fact that the right to education should be guaranteed and respected, both sides are committed to maintaining a conducive academic environment in the educational institutions. Both sides agree to guarantee that the right to education would not be impeded. They agree to put to an end, on an immediate basis, activities like taking the educational institutions under control and using them, abducting teachers and students, taking them under control and making them to disappear, and not to establish barracks in a way that it would impede them.

7.5.5. Both sides agree that the private property of any individual would not be seized or usurped, except permitted by the laws.

7.5.6. Both sides believe in the fact that the industrial climate in the country should not be disturbed and production should be given continuity and that the right of collective bargaining and social security should be respected. They also believe in the fact that if any problem arises between the business houses and labourers, they should be encouraged to resolve the problem in a peaceful manner. Both sides respect the right to work prescribed by the International Labour Organisation.

7.6. *Women and Child Rights:*

7.6.1. Both sides fully agree to protect the rights of the

women and children in a special way, to immediately stop all types of violence against women and children, including child labour as well as sexual exploitation and abuse. They also fully agree not to include or use children, who are 18 years old and below in the armed force. Children thus affected would be instantaneously rescued and necessary and suitable assistance would be provided for their rehabilitation.

7.7. *Right of Personal Liberty:*

7.7.1. Both sides agree to the freedom of opinion and expression; freedom to assemble peaceably and without arms; freedom of movement; freedom to practice any profession, or to carry on any occupation, industry or trade; press and publication rights; the freedom to take part in peaceful political activities; the right of equality before the law; and to implement and have a tolerable system of justice implemented.

8. Dispute Settlement and Implementation Mechanism

8.1. Both sides agree to become responsible and accountable in a personal and collective way and not to repeat in future mistakes committed in the past and also to correct these mistakes on a gradual basis.

8.2. The National Peace and Rehabilitation Commission can set up mechanism as per the need for making the campaign for peace successful. The composition and working procedures of the Commission would be as determined by the interim Council of Ministers.

8.3. Both sides are committed to settle all kinds of present or possible future mutual differences or problems through mutual talks, understanding, consensus and dialogue.

8.4. Both sides express commitment that the interim Council of Ministers can constitute and determine the working procedures of the National Peace and Rehabilitation Commission, the Truth and Reconciliation

Commission, the High-level State Restructuring Recommendation Commission and other mechanisms as per the need to implement this agreement, the Interim Constitution and all the decisions, agreements and understandings reached between the Seven-party Alliance, the Government of Nepal and the CPN (Maoist).

9. IMPLEMENTATION AND FOLLOW-UP

Both sides have agreed to make the following arrangements for the implementation of the understandings mentioned in this agreement and for their follow-up:

9.1. Both sides agree to give continuity to the task of monitoring of the human rights provisions mentioned in this agreement by the United Nations Office of the High Commissioner for Human Rights, Nepal.

9.2. Both sides agree for the monitoring of the management of arms and the armies by the United Nations Mission in Nepal as mentioned in the five-point letter sent to the UN earlier and in the present agreement.

9.3. Both sides agree to get the United Nations supervise the election to the Constituent Assembly.

9.4. The National Human Rights Commission shall also carry out works related to the monitoring of human rights as mentioned in this agreement together with the responsibility assigned to it as per the laws. In connection with carrying out its works, the Commission can take the help of national and international human rights organisations after maintaining necessary coordination with them.

9.5. Both sides agree to accept the reports submitted by the above-mentioned bodies, to provide the information requested by them, and to implement the suggestions and recommendations given by them on the basis of consensus and dialogue.

10. Miscellaneous

10.1. Both sides agree not to operate parallel or any form of structure in any areas of the state or government structure as per the letter of the decisions of November 8 and the spirit of the peace agreement.

10.2. Both sides accept to sign any complementary agreements, as necessitated, for the implementation of the present agreement.

10.3. This agreement can be revised any time with the consent of both sides. Both sides agree to provide to each other prior written information if they wish to make any changes. The amendments could be made to the agreement with the consent of both sides after receiving the information. The provisions to be made by such an amendment would not be below the minimum standards of the accepted international human rights and humanitarian laws.

10.4. If any disputes arise in any interpretation of this agreement, a joint mechanism comprising both sides shall make the interpretation on the basis of the preamble and the documents included in the schedule of this agreement, and this interpretation would be final.

10.5. The concept of 'two sides' as mentioned in this agreement would automatically cease to exist after the constitution of the Interim Legislature — Parliament. Thereafter, all the responsibility of implementing the obligations stated in this agreement shall be as per the arrangements made by the interim Council of Ministers. It would be the duty and responsibility of all the political parties to extend cooperation in the compliance and implementation of the agreement.

10.6. We heartily appeal to one and all to extend cooperation for resolving their problems and demands through talks and dialogue and for holding the election to the constituent assembly and maintaining the law and order, at a time when the entire country is focused on the main campaign of the election of the Constituent Assembly.

10.7. We heartily appeal to the civil society, the professional groups, the class organisations, the media, the intellectual community and all the Nepali people to actively participate in this historic campaign of building a new Nepal and establishing lasting peace through the election of the Constituent Assembly by ending the armed conflict.

10.8. We heartily urge all the friendly countries and the United Nations, as well as the International Community to extend support to Nepal in this campaign of establishing full democracy and lasting peace.

Cognizant of the responsibility of the future of the country and the people, and becoming fully committed to this comprehensive peace agreement, we, on behalf of the Government of Nepal and the Communist Party of Nepal (Maoist), hereby make public this comprehensive peace agreement after signing it.

Prachanda :	Girija Prasad Koirala
President :	Prime Minister
Communist Party of Nepal (Maoist) :	Government of Nepal
Signed on November 21, 2006	

Annexure 13

Agreement on Monitoring of Management of Arms and Armies on November 28, 2006

Preamble

In keeping with the letters to the United Nations (UN) Secretary-General of 9 August and the Comprehensive Peace Accord of 21 November 2006;

Guaranteeing the fundamental right of the Nepali people to take part in the constituent assembly elections in a free and fair environment without fear;

Declaring the beginning of a new chapter of peaceful democratic interaction by ending the armed conflict taking place in the country since 1996, based on the Comprehensive Peace Accord between the two parties in order to accomplish, through the constituent assembly, certainty of sovereignty of the Nepali people, progressive political outlet, democratic restructuring of the state, and social-economic-cultural transformation; and,

Affirming the will to fully observe the terms of this bilateral agreement witnessed by the United Nations:

The parties agree to seek UN assistance in monitoring the management of the arms and armies of both sides by the deployment of qualified UN civilian personnel to monitor, according to international norms, the confinement of Maoist army combatants and their weapons within designated cantonment areas and monitor the Nepal Army (NA) to ensure that it remains in its barracks and its weapons are not used against any side.

Modalities of the Agreement

Principles

Neither of the parties shall engage in movement or redeployment of forces resulting in tactical or strategic advantage.

Any claims or reports of violations of this agreement will be reported to the UN monitors, substantiated or not substantiated, and subsequently reported to the parties through the appropriate representative of the UN Mission in Nepal.

The security forces deployed by the interim government shall have authority to conduct routine patrol, explore in order to prevent illegal trafficking of the weapons, explosives or raw materials used in assembling weapons at the international border or custom points and seize them.

Both parties agree to allow the United Nations, international donor agencies and diplomatic missions based in Nepal, national and international non-governmental organizations, press, human rights activists, election observers and foreign tourists to travel unrestricted according to law in the state of Nepal. The parties will respect the security, freedom of movement and well-being of UN Mission and associated staff, goods and services in all parts of Nepal.

The parties shall immediately take all necessary measures to cooperate with efforts aimed at controlling illicit trafficking of arms and the infiltration of armed groups.

Both parties fully agree to not include or use children who are 18 years old and under in the armed forces. Children thus affected would be immediately rescued and necessary and appropriate assistance will be provided for their rehabilitation.

Definitions

The following definitions are accepted:

(1) Cantonment (Maoist army) is a temporarily designated and clearly defined geographical area for encampment and

provision of services for the Maoist combatant units including weapons, ammunition and equipment. The cantonments are provided for all echelons of the Maoist army.

(2) Barracking (NA) is the deployment of Nepal Army units to barracks, including weapons, ammunition and equipment. No units below a company level will be independently deployed unless for activities specified elsewhere in this agreement or otherwise mutually agreed by the parties.

(3) Secure arms storage areas are either military barracks with regular armoury stores used for storage of weapons, munitions and explosives, or storage containers established in special perimeters at cantonment sites controlled and guarded by the responsible unit.

(4) "The parties" refers to the party of Government of Nepal (including the Nepal Army) and the party of the Communist Party of Nepal (Maoist), (including the Maoist Army).

(5) UN Monitoring refers to all efforts by the United Nations to determine relative compliance with the terms spelled out in this agreement and to report to all the parties and others concerned its findings.

(6) The Joint Monitoring Coordination Committee (JMCC) is the monitoring, reporting and coordinating body chaired by the UN with membership of the parties. The JMCC is responsible for supervising compliance by the parties to this agreement.

(7) Joint Monitoring Teams (JMTs) are the bodies, which will assist in monitoring the cessation of hostilities. The Joint Monitoring Teams will be active at the regional and local levels and in mobile teams. Each team will be comprised of one UN monitor serving as team leader, one monitor from Nepal Army and one monitor from the Maoist Army. Joint Monitoring Teams will not be used for weapons storage inspections. Inspections at Maoist army cantonments will take place with a UN monitoring team and a representative of the Maoist army. Inspections at Nepal Army barracks will

take place with a UN monitoring team and a Nepal Army representative.

(8) Maoist army combatants: For purposes of this agreement this will include regular active duty members of the Maoist army, who joined service before 25 May 2006, who are not minors and who are able to demonstrate their service, including by CPN(M) identity card and other means agreed by the parties.

Promotion

The parties shall promote awareness of this agreement, and adherence to its provisions, among their commanders, members and affiliated groups.

The parties, Government of Nepal, Nepal Army (NA), CPN (M) and the Maoist army, shall design, in cooperation with the UN Mission, an awareness programme to ensure that local communities and the parties' commanders, members and affiliated groups understand the mandate of the UN Mission and all of the obligations of the parties spelled out in this agreement. The information programmes shall include the use of meetings and print and electronic media in local languages.

Phases

This agreement shall come into force upon signing. These phases shall occur in the following sequence:

(1) Reporting and verification;
(2) Redeployment and concentration of forces;
(3) Maoist army cantonment, NA barracking and arms control; and
(4) Full compliance with the agreement.

A full and practical timeline will be established by the parties for all of these activities to take place in consultation with the UN.

1. Reporting and Verification

The parties will report detailed information about their troops and this information will be treated with appropriate confidentiality by the United Nations. The parties will provide maps and sketches showing current dispositions, including:

(1) Order of battle/military structure, organisation, deployment and number of troops;
(2) Minefields, landmines, unexploded ordnance, standard explosives, improvised explosive devices and exact location of such items;
(3) All necessary information about roads, tracks, trails and passages related to encampments;
(4) Information regarding armed or unarmed groups working along with the parties, the Nepal Army (NA) and the Maoist army, including their responsibilities; and
(5) Other information required by the UN for proper monitoring of the disposition of arms and armies.

The UN Mission shall check this information immediately after monitors are deployed.

2. Redeployment and Concentration of Forces

Comprehensive plans, timelines and routes for the redeployment and concentration of forces will be provided by both the NA and Maoist army to the UN Mission.

The redeployment and concentration of all combatants in Nepal — with the NA in barracks and the Maoist army moving in to cantonment sites — shall be carried out in consultation with the UN. The redeployment and cantonment of forces will be monitored by the UN monitors after they are deployed.

Both sides express an understanding to create a record of government, public and private buildings, land and other properties and return them immediately.

The parties will withdraw all military and paramilitary checkpoints (unless explicitly permitted in this agreement) to promote and guarantee free movement and create an environment free of fear and intimidation.

The Nepal Police and Armed Police Force shall continue the task of maintaining law and order and conduct criminal investigations as per the spirit and sentiment of the Jana Andolan and peace accord as well as the prevailing law. Both parties agree not to operate parallel or other forms of mechanism in any areas of the state or state machinery as per the spirit of the decisions of November 8, 2006 and the essence of the peace accord. All sides agree to let employees of Nepal Government and public agencies travel freely to any part of the country, to fulfil their duties and not to create any obstacle or obstruction while executing their work or not to let obstructions to arise and to facilitate their work.

3. Maoist Army Cantonment, Barracking of the NA and Arms Control

Maoist army Cantonment

In accordance with the commitment expressed in the letter sent to the United Nations, Maoist army combatants and their weapons shall be confined within designated cantonment areas. The cantonment shall be based on comprehensive planning and preparation before implementation. After the Maoist army combatants stay in the temporary cantonments, the Government of Nepal will provide food supplies and other necessary arrangements. When implemented, the comprehensive concept shall ensure good communications and proper logistics. UN monitors will have access to any and all cantonment sites for purposes of monitoring.

Commanders' Responsibilities

The normal Maoist army chain of command, control, communication and information will be utilised to control the Maoist army cantonment, using the normal Maoist army structure in administration of the sites.

There will be seven main cantonment sites and 21 satellite cantonment sites of three per main cantonment site. The satellite sites will be clustered no more than two hours driving distance from the main sites unless otherwise agreed by the parties.

The designated seven main sites will be under command, control, communication and information of the Maoist army site commander and the satellite sites by the designated satellite commanders. The site commanders shall provide the following information in detail for each site to the UN Mission:

(1) Command structure for the unit and sub-units plotted on a map;
(2) Names of commanders down to company level;
(3) Communication system;
(4) Complete list of personnel;
(5) Complete list of weapons, i.e. types, numbers, serial numbers and calibre under storage at the main cantonment sites;
(6) Ammunition inventory type, lot number and amount; and
(7) List of names for the site security guards detachment, and complete list of weapons and ammunition for the detachment (main and satellite cantonment levels).

Site commanders' responsibilities include:

(1) Camp security, including access control to the site;
(2) Respect of the security, freedom of movement and well-being of UN and associated staff, goods and services;
(3) Providing information in cooperation with the UN Mission;
(4) Maintenance of discipline, morale and normal training in the spirit of the Comprehensive Peace Accord, excluding live fire exercises;

(5) Daily routines and control of troops; and

(6) Logistics and camp services (in cooperation with the Government of Nepal and other assisting agencies).

Weapons Storage and Control

The parties agree upon the safe storage of all Maoist army weapons and ammunition, in the seven main cantonment areas under UN monitoring, except as provided below for perimeter security purposes. Both sides shall assist each other to mark landmines and booby-traps used during the time of armed conflict by providing necessary information within 30 days and to defuse and remove/lift and destroy them within 60 days. All improvised explosive devices will be collected at designated sites a safe distance from the main cantonment areas. Unsuitable devices will be destroyed immediately. Stable devices will be stored safely and under 24-hour armed guard. The parties, in consultation with the UN, will determine a timeline and process for the later destruction of all improvised explosive devices. To ensure the safety of both monitors and Maoist army personnel, no improvised explosive devices or crude bombs will be brought inside the cantonment sites.

In the main cantonment sites, the weapons and ammunition storage area will be secured by the following system:

(1) A solid fence will surround the specified area, including a gate with a lock. There will be signs on the fence clearly identifying the restricted area.

(2) The weapons storage depot will be composed of storage containers painted white and furnished with shelves for safe weapons storage and easy control, and with a complete inventory (weapon type, calibre and serial number).

(3) A single lock provided by the UN will secure each storage container. The key will be held by the designated main cantonment site commander. A 24-hour surveillance camera will cover the storage site and will be monitored from the

UN office in the cantonment site. Floodlights will be switched on automatically during hours of darkness.

(4) The UN will provide an inspection registration device mounted on each container door indicating when the storage container has been opened.

(5) An alarm system will be connected to sirens in both the UN office and the camp commander's office. The system will be activated if the container door is opened without a "safe button" having been switched off in connection with regular inspections.

(6) UN monitors will carry out the inspections of the arms storage area and containers in the presence of a Maoist army representative.

Each main cantonment site will be allowed 30 weapons of the same make and model to be used only for clearly defined perimeter security by designated guards, with each satellite allowed 15 such weapons under the same conditions. These weapons will all be properly registered with make and serial number and locked in a guardhouse when not in use. The parties, in consultation with the UN, will periodically review the number of weapons needed for perimeter security purposes on the basis of a shared threat assessment.

Security provisions will be made for CPN (M) leaders through understanding with the government. The UN Mission shall monitor these commitments with a full-time presence at the Maoist army main cantonment sites and through field visits and regular inspections. These inspections will be carried out randomly and without warning.

Registration of Maoist Army Combatants at Cantonment Sites

All Maoist army combatants will be registered at the main cantonment sites. This registration will include the provision of age, name, rank, responsibilities within unit/formation, date of entry into service and will provide the basis for a complete list of personnel. Maoist combatants will be registered regardless if they are in possession of weapons or not. If with weapon, the type and condition of weapon will be specified. The total number of weapons will be categorized by unit/formation. Only those individuals, who were members of the Maoist army before 25 May 2006, will be eligible for cantonment. The parties will agree as to how this pre-existing service is to be confirmed in consultation with the UN.

As part of this registration, all Maoist army combatants will present their Maoist army identity card to be marked by the UN. The process for marking the cards will be determined. This registration card will be the basis for any assistance received by Maoist army members. Unregistered persons will not be eligible for assistance or permitted to remain in cantonments.

Only those Maoist army combatants, who have been properly registered at cantonment sites, will be eligible for possible integration into the security forces fulfilling the standard norms. Any discharged personnel will be ineligible for possible integration. Those who are eligible for integration into the security forces will be determined by a special committee as agreed in the Comprehensive Peace Accord. This integration process will be determined in subsequent agreement with the parties.

Upon registration, Maoist army combatants, if found to be born after 25 May 1988, will be honourably and automatically discharged.

Discharged Maoist army combatants must: release all weapons, uniforms and other military gear; and, agree not to return to cantonment sites unless mutually agreed by UN monitors in consultation with the parties. The assistance packages to be provided to voluntarily discharged personnel will be agreed by the parties in advance of cantonment.

The Interim Council of Ministers will form a special committee to supervise, integrate and rehabilitate the Maoist army combatants.

Barracking of the Nepal Army

General Regulations

In accordance with the commitment expressed in the letter sent to the United Nations, the Nepal Army shall remain in its barracks and its arms are not to be used in favour of or against any side. UN monitors will have access to any and all NA barracks for purposes of monitoring whether Nepal Army forces or weapons are being used for or against any party. Upon visiting any Nepal Army barracks for inspection, the site commander will be duly notified, and UN inspections will relate only to matters regarding the disposition of forces and weapons.

The Council of Ministers will control, mobilise and manage the Nepal Army as per the Army Act of 2006 (Sainik Ain 2063) or its successor legislation. The Interim Council of Ministers to prepare and implement the detailed action plan of the Nepal Army's democratization by taking suggestions from the concerned committee of the Interim Parliament/legislature. Under this to carry out activities like assessing the appropriate number of the Nepal Army, to train the army in democratic and human rights values while developing democratic structure, national and inclusive character.

Commander Responsibilities

The normal NA chain of command, control, communication and information will be utilised to monitor the NA deployment to barracks. The commanders shall provide the following information in detail to the UN Mission:

(1) Command structure for the unit and sub-units plotted on a map;
(2) Names of commanders down to company level;
(3) Communication system;
(4) Order of battle/military structure, organisation, deployment and number of troops;
(5) Minefields, landmines, unexploded ordnance, standard explosives, improvised explosive devices and exact location of such items; and
(6) Other information required by the UN for proper monitoring of the disposition of arms and armies.

The NA will respect the security, freedom of movement and well-being of UN and associated staff, goods and services, and provide information in cooperation with the UN Mission according to Section 2.

The UN Mission shall monitor these commitments through daily presence in selected NA barracks, field visits and regular inspections.

Weapons Storage and Control

The Nepal Army will remain within the barracks as per the commitment expressed in the letter sent to the UN to ensure that their arms are not used for or against any party. The Nepal Army to store arms in equal numbers to that of the Maoist army, to seal it with a single-lock and give the key to the concerned party. In the process of installing the lock, to assemble a mechanism including a siren and register for the monitoring by the UN. While carrying out the necessary examination of the stored arms, the UN will do so under the presence of the concerned party. The barrack where NA arms will be monitored under the conditions spelled out in section 4.1.2 will be identified and agreed by the parties. The arms will be stored in storage containers.

Deployment and Concentration of Forces — NA Permitted Activities

In accordance with the spirit of the Comprehensive Peace Accord, continuity will be given to functions of the Nepal Army including border security, security of the conservation areas, protected areas, banks, airports, power houses, telephone towers, central secretariat and security of VIPs. A detailed list of these institutions and installations will be kept by the NA, along with the number and types of forces assigned to such duties. The list of such institutions and installations will be kept by the NA under seal, and this information will be made available to UN monitors when deemed necessary in a case-by-case basis.

Permitted NA activities include:

1. Routine military activities within the barracks and regular training in barracks and camps. The JMCC will be notified 48 hours in advance before undertaking limited live fire exercises at designated live firing ranges.
2. Participation in official ceremonies, parades, etc. as directed by the Government.
3. Provision of Border Security as directed by the Government.
4. Relief of troops on a one-to-one basis, including transport as mentioned.
5. Regular maintenance and replacement of non-lethal equipment, including transport as mentioned. Maintenance and replacement of lethal weapons will take place only with the determination of the interim government or agreement by both parties.
6. Execution of development and construction tasks as directed by the civilian authorities, at central, regional and local levels.
7. Provision of support in relief work in times of natural and other disasters as directed by the Government.
8. Participation in Peacekeeping Operations called for by the United Nations, and all preparations, transport, training, transfer of equipment, etc. connected to this.
9. Provision of security for VVIPs and VIPs.
10. Provision of security of vital installations as directed by the Government.
11. Provision of security of transportation of Nepal Rastra Bank funds.

For all of the above activities, the rules regarding notification of troop, air movements and exercises spelled out in section 5.2 apply.

4. Compliance with the Agreement

Prohibited Activities

In the spirit of the Comprehensive Peace Accord, and in light of this agreement, after the placement of the Nepal Army in the barracks and the Maoist Army combatants in cantonment, the parties shall scrupulously refrain from the following activities:

1. Holding and carrying arms is in violation of the law. Displaying arms, intimidation and any type of use of violence is prohibited, and use of arms is legally punishable.
2. Any type of arms and weapons targeted against each other in a direct or indirect way or any act of attack.
3. Harming or intimidating any person, including internally displaced persons, humanitarian and development workers and other non-combatants, and any seizure of their equipment and property.
4. Ambushes, murder or violent operations.
5. Kidnapping, unlawful detention or imprisonment, disappearances.
6. All offensive military flights in and over Nepal.
7. Damaging or seizing public/private/government, military or UN property and all attacks on UN personnel and installations.
8. Planting mines or improvised explosive devices, conducting sabotage or military espionage.
9. Recruiting additional armed forces or conducting military activities against each other, including transporting weapons, ammunitions and explosives (unless mutually agreed by the parties and notified in advance according to the terms of this agreement).
10. Collecting cash or goods and services or levying tax against one's wishes and against the existing law.

11. Any actions that impede or delay the provision of humanitarian assistance or protection to civilians.
12. Any restrictions on the safe, free and unimpeded movement of humanitarian or development agencies undertaking activities approved by the interim government or its successor.
13. All acts and forms of gender-based violence.
14. Any restrictions on the free movement of people and goods.
15. All activities that obstruct the efforts of the UN Mission and amount to a failure to cooperate with the UN Mission, including the prohibition of the UN Mission patrols and flights over any location.
16. Any attempt by a party to disguise its equipment, personnel or activities as those of the UN Mission, other United Nations agencies, the International Committee of the Red Cross/Crescent or any other similar organisation.
17. Any attempt to redeploy military forces and equipment or occupation of any positions out of their respective deployment positions without the consent of the Joint Monitoring Coordination Committee.
18. The use of children who are 18 years old and under in the armed forces.
19. All hostile propaganda and incitement to military action.
20. The parties shall also refrain from all activities that are prohibited elsewhere in this agreement.

Permitted Activities

The key principle that shall underpin permitted activities for both sides shall be to alleviate the effects of the armed conflict on civilians and the war-affected areas and to galvanise popular support for peace. Permitted activities for both sides will be conducted as per the decisions of the interim government. Troop, air movements and exercises have to be properly notified and approved by the Joint Monitoring Coordination Committee at least 48-hours in advance.

Permitted activities include:

(1) De-mining and decommissioning of military hazards;
(2) Development activities to include improvement and opening of roads, rehabilitation of bridges and passages and airstrips according to the decisions of the interim government;
(3) Humanitarian relief;
(4) Socio-economic activities such as assisting free movement of people, goods and services;
(5) Free movement of unarmed soldiers in plain civilian clothes, who are on granted leave, medical referrals, or visiting families — no more than 12 per cent of the total retained force at a given cantonment or barracks will be on authorised leave at any given time unless mutually agreed by the parties;
(6) Supply of non-lethal items to military units, food, water, medicine, petrol, oil and lubricants, stationary, uniforms etc; and
(7) Medical evacuation.

Violations

The following acts shall constitute violations of the agreement:

(1) Any act that contravenes this agreement;
(2) Unauthorised troop movements;
(3) Unauthorised recruitment, conscription or mobilisation;
(4) Unauthorised replenishment of military equipment;
(5) Violation of human rights, humanitarian law or obstruction of freedom of movement of people, goods and services;
(6) Espionage, sabotage, air surveillance and acts of subversion; and
(7) Military flights, or military flights utilising civilian aircraft, over cantonment sites without 48-hour notification to the parties and the UN mission, except in emergency situations or medical evacuations.

The United Nations Mission

The Joint Monitoring Coordination Committee

The Joint Monitoring Coordination Committee (JMCC), the chairman of which will be appointed by the UN mission and the delegates from the parties will be determined by the parties themselves. The nine-member JMCC shall be composed of representatives from the UN, NA and Maoist Army. The neutral Chairman will be appointed by the United Nations. There will be two Vice-Chairmen, one each from the Maoist Army and the NA. The remaining six members will be two UN, two NA and two Maoist army, all as selected by the parties.

The JMCC shall reach its decisions by consensus. In the event of a deadlock, the representative of the UN Secretary-General shall have final authority for reporting on the compliance of the parties with this agreement to the Secretary-General and to the interim government for resolution. The Chairman shall report regularly to the representative of the Secretary-General and to the designated representatives of the parties regarding the activities of the JMCC.

The JMCC shall serve three main functions:

(1) To assist the parties in implementing this agreement. The JMCC shall be the central coordinating body for monitoring arms and armies in accordance with the terms of this agreement.

(2) To serve as a dispute resolution mechanism. The JMCC shall resolve all disputes and military or operational difficulties, complaints, questions or problems regarding implementation of this agreement.

(3) To assist in confidence building. The JMCC shall work to gain the trust and confidence of the parties and promote the overall goals of this agreement among the people in Nepal.

In order to achieve these goals, the JMCC shall operate according to the following basic principles:

(1) Resolve all problems and disputes at the lowest level possible, i.e. delegation of authority to the JMTs;
(2) Promote joint problem-solving and build trust and confidence through active efforts to appropriately investigate and report on all incidents of concern to the parties; and
(3) Build on lessons learned in the process.

The Joint Monitoring Teams (JMTs) will assist the Joint Monitoring Coordination Committee at the local level and through site visits. The JMTs will comprise one international monitor as the team leader and one monitor from Nepal Army and one monitor from the Maoist Army. The number of JMTs and their deployment will be determined by the chair of the JMCC in consultations with that body.

The tasks of the JMTs will include:

(1) Village and community visits and liaison with the civilian community;
(2) Cooperation with other UN-agencies, and liaison with international organisations and non-governmental organisations;
(3) Assistance to the parties in creating a favourable operational environment for the conduct of the ceasefire by information sharing and defusing local tension;
(4) A pro-active concept for initiation of conflict management at the local level; and
(5) Investigation of complaints linked to possible alleged violations of the agreement, reference paragraph 5.1, and to recommend measures to ensure compliance.

Miscellaneous

This agreement can be revised at any time with the consent of both parties. Both parties agree to provide to each other prior written information if they wish to make any change. The amendments can be made to the agreement with the consent of both parties after receiving the information. The provisions to be made by such an amendment will not fall below the minimum standards of accepted international human rights and humanitarian laws.

Both parties consent to sign any complementary understandings, as necessary, for the implementation of the present agreement.

This agreement will be signed by both parties in Nepali and English. The United Nations will witness the English language version of this agreement and, accordingly, the English-language version of this agreement will be considered as authoritative in matters of dispute.

The spirit of the Comprehensive Peace Accord shall guide the interpretation and implementation of this agreement by all the parties.

Done in Kathmandu, Nepal on the 28th day of November, 2006 (12 Mangsir 2063 BS)

Krishna B. Mahara	Krishna P. Sitaula
Coordinator	*Coordinator*
Negotiating team	Negotiating team
CPN (Maoist)	Government of Nepal

Witnessed by
Ian Martin
Personal Representative of the Secretary-General
United Nations

Annexure 14

May 28, 2008 Declaration of Republic by the House of Representatives

Respecting the popular mandate given by the Nepalese people through the historic struggles, revolutions and People's Movements launched time and again by them since 1951, in order to institutionalise the achievements, embracing the onus commissioned through the agreements concluded between political parties and Article 159 (2) of Nepal's Interim Constitution 2007, the Government of Nepal tables the following proposal at the first meeting of the Constituent Assembly for the implementation of republic:

1) This first meeting of the Constituent Assembly duly announces transformation of the independent, indivisible, sovereign, secular and inclusive Nepal into a federal democratic republic, with sovereignty and state power being vested in Nepalese people.
2) As the nation has been duly promulgated a democratic republic, all constitutional provisions, laws and administrative provisions shall be deemed null and void to the extent they are inconsistent with them. The laws, traditions, customs, social and cultural practices as well as all prevalent rights, facilities, status and awards granted to the then King and members of his family distinct from common Nepalese citizens shall automatically stand rescinded.
3) At a time when Nepal has been duly declared a federal democratic republic, necessary bill for amendment of Nepal's Interim Constitution has been tabled to constitutionally institutionalize the indispensable provisions, including the provision on President. Another bill shall be tabled on the

amendment of other matters, including presidential election system.

4) On the historic occasion of Nepal's transformation into a federal democratic republic heralding a new era, this meeting pays heartfelt tribute to all known and unknown martyrs. On this occasion, heartily felicitating all Nepalese people, this meeting heartily appeals all Nepalese within and outside the country to joyously celebrate Jestha 15 as Republic Day from today and every year thereafter.

5) In the context of Nepal having been proclaimed a democratic republic, the Government of Nepal will make necessary provisions for using the premises of the Narayanhiti Royal Palace and the entire heritage within it in national interest, including as a historical museum.

Annexure 15

The 7-Point Agreement on the future of the PLA

(Signed by four major parties
[UCPN-Maoist, Nepali Congress, CPN-UML and Samyukta Madhesi Morcha]
on November 1, 2011).

1. Integration and Rehabilitation of People's Liberation Army (PLA)

a) Details of cantoned PLA soldiers will be updated,

b) The number of PLA soldiers to be integrated in the Nepal Army will be 6,500. The integration will be in the Directorate under the NA, comprising 65 per cent from the security body and 35 per cent from the PLA. The functions of the Directorate will be in the fields of development-construction, forest security, industrial security and disaster management.

c) The PLA soldiers opting for integration will meet standards of the security body concerned on, individual basis. But, flexibility shall be adopted in age (by 3 years) and education (by 1 level) and the marital status of the entrants.

d) Ranks of the enlisted soldiers will be determined based on the standards of the security body, concerned. The ranking will take place on the basis of the existing system of the security body, and without affecting the career growth of those already serving under the security body concerned. The enrolment date of the PLA soldiers will be based on the date, previously recorded by the verification of UNMIN.

e) The integrated soldiers will join the assigned service under the stipulated ranks only after completing the bridging course and trainings.

f) All weapons under the PLA will automatically come under the jurisdiction of the government after the beginning of the integration process.

2. Rehabilitation of PLA Combatants

a) PLA soldiers up for rehabilitation will be provided with an alternative package deal for education, training and professional opportunities. The rehabilitation fund will range from Rs. 600,000 to Rs. 900,000.

b) PLA soldiers, who voluntarily resign from their posts in lieu of monetary exchange, will receive Rs. 800,000, Rs. 700,000, Rs. 600,000 and Rs. 500,000, respectively based on the ranks of the resigning soldiers. The distribution will be made in two instalments in two fiscal years. Official decision in this regard will be taken by the Special Committee in two days.

3. Group Division

a) The special committee will decide on the procedural issues pertaining to the integration and rehabilitation processes in seven days, thus starting the group division that shall conclude within November 23, 2011.

4. Formation of Commissions as per Consensus

a) Bills concerning Truth and Reconciliation Commission and Commission for Investigation of the Disappeared will be endorsed by parliament on the basis of consensus. The commissions will be formed within one month.

b) Conflict-era cases will be dealt with as per the spirit of the Comprehensive Peace Agreement and the Interim Constitution.

5. Relief Aid for Conflict Victims

a) Relief aid will be provided to families of those killed, injured, maimed, disappeared and displaced in the conflict.

6. Forging of a Trustworthy Environment for the Implementation of Past Agreements

a) UCPN (Maoist) shall return all property seized or occupied by the party to rightful owners within November 23, 2011. With the return of the land, the owners will be given appropriate compensation.

b) Farmers' rights will be ensured as per the spirit of the CPA, Interim Constitution and scientific land reform system.

c) The structure and functions of the Maoist-affiliated Young Communist League (YCL) will be demobilised, while all private and public buildings and land occupied by the YCL will be vacated within November 23, 2011.

d) Vehicles used by the UCPN (Maoist) as registered at the Department of Transport Management will be legalised within November 23, 2011. Illegal vehicles will be impounded.

e) Local administration will monitor and implement the agreement pertaining to the return of the seized property.

7. Drafting of Constitution and Formation of National Consensus Government

a) Dialogue among political parties will continue to assist the peace building and constitution drafting processes. A high level political mechanism will be formed in this regard.

b) Work related to constitution drafting will be accelerated. The Constituent Assembly will form a panel of experts to take suggestions on the issue of state restructuring. Work for the preparation of a draft constitution will begin in one month.

c) Process for formation of a national consensus government will begin once peace building and constitution drafting processes pick momentum.

Index